# SPANIEL TRAINING
## for Modern Shooters

*Books of related interest*

# SPANIEL TRAINING

## for

## Modern Shooters

## MAURICE HOPPER

DAVID & CHARLES
Newton Abbot    London    Vancouver

0 7153 6446 4

First published 1974
Second impression 1978

Printed in Great Britain
by Redwood Burn Ltd  Trowbridge & Esher
for David & Charles (Publishers) Limited
Brunel House  Newton Abbot  Devon

Published in Canada by
Douglas David & Charles Limited
1875 Welch Street  North Vancouver  BC

To the shooting men with whom I have had so much good sport, in the hope that they may find even more pleasure henceforth in the company of dogs of which they can be proud; to my fellow professionals, from whom I have learned so much; and to all the spaniels I have trained, for they have taught me more than I taught them.

# CONTENTS

# LIST OF ILLUSTRATIONS

# ACKNOWLEDGEMENTS

Over the years several people have helped me in a practical way and with advice. When I joined the staff of the War Dogs Training School in the early forties that very experienced trainer Reg Hill was our instructor and we learned much from him. And it was while I was on the staff that I met two friends who have helped me immeasurably. The first of these was Bill Adams, alsatian trainer par excellence, and his advice has helped me throughout my training career.

The other friend on the staff to whom I am referring was Jack Chudley, the great professional trainer, who needs no introduction to anyone connected with gundogs. Apart from the practical help that Jack has given me during the post-war years the value of his advice has been incalculable. Space precludes me from listing details but I learned from him about the sequence of training, and what I have referred to as 'the three ball trick'. These are but two bits of guidance amongst many. It is a debt I cannot repay.

I have been lucky in other friends and mention three. The late Colonel Carrell, with whom I began my career, introduced me to Spaniel training. Two neighbouring sporting farmers, Cliff Butler and Percy Selby, have allowed me to train on their land.

My wife, Judith, with practical help and much patience has made much possible which otherwise would not have been.

The pictures of spaniels in training were taken by John Tarlton, and that of Field Trial Champion Lytchmore Hamers Jean by S. F. James.

# *FOREWORD*

Maurice Hopper is a senior member of the small, dedicated circle of professional gundog trainers. From his Dorset kennel he has produced a succession of efficient, mannerly dogs for his circle of clients. On them and on himself he imposes conditions, accepting for training only those dogs which by breeding and character are likely to develop into satisfactory shooting companions, and never accepting more than he can teach on an individual basis.

In recent years the word has gone round, for unascertainable reasons, that spaniels have a more headstrong temperament than retrievers and can be handled only by those of exceptional talent or enthusiasm. In my experience this is not so. It is true that, being more active and versatile, the contrast between a well-trained spaniel and a wild one is apt to be more spectacularly demonstrated than would be the case among the more sedentary retrievers. It is not true that ill manners are likely in a spaniel if the animal is well bred to the gun, if it is properly educated, and if it is worked by a sportsman who pays as much attention to his dog work as to his shooting. Nor is it true, as is sometimes implied, that spaniel training demands of the trainer any special physical activity and even athletic endeavour in coming to terms with a boisterous and occasionally mutinous type of animal.

The facts indicate otherwise. What we now know as English Springer Spaniels have been bred generation after generation for hundreds of years to the special service to man. Before modern shotguns were invented they served the originators of 'shooting flying'. Before muzzle-loaders were invented they sprang game for the falconers, and drove duck and waders into fowlers' nets. They were certainly doing this in the reigns of the Norman kings, and possibly during the Roman occupation. From all these centuries comes an inherent desire to do man's wishes—if only man will come to terms with the desire and learn to communicate his wishes.

Mr Hopper lost a leg in battle in Holland. With diminished mobility he is denied the capability to train a dog by any principles other than developing and guiding its wish to serve man, and especially a man with a gun (not that other principles are of any use). The methods he has evolved have been developed over the years into perfectionism. His canine pupils learn not only the skills of shooting dogs, but the manners which permit them to be welcomed and to move confidently in human society. His aim is to produce not mere servants, but helpful companions whose presence will make good days better wherever men may shoot.

Wilson Stephens
Editor, *The Field*

*Chapter 1*

# UNDERSTANDING

Whenever I send a puppy away by rail there is a label on the box saying, 'Valuable Live puppy. Please handle with care.' It is sad but true that there are still far too few gundogs that are really handled throughout their working lives with the care that they deserve. It is an open secret that the most common of sayings amongst professional gundog trainers is that the owners need training as much, or more, than their dogs. After nearly forty years practical experience as a trainer, I have no valid reason to dispute this.

This refers, of course, to those owners who have their dogs professionally trained, with the implication that they do not have the necessary knowledge, experience, or time, to maintain the standard of behaviour to which their dogs had originally been trained. But if there are still so many people who lack the know-how to do the comparatively simple job of keeping a well-trained dog up to standard, how many more are there who do not know how to train a dog to a high standard on their own account. Judging by the behaviour of most spaniels in the shooting field, there are a great many people who do

13

not have much idea at all. I have attended a great many shoots and, occasionally, it has been my pleasure to watch some really good work by well-behaved dogs that had patently received the correct training initially and were handled by shooting men who knew how to work their dogs to the best advantage. But for every well-behaved dog of this calibre I have seen at least thirty whose behaviour varied from bad to atrocious. Dogs that were unsteady and completely out of hand, and dogs that totally ignored every command. Dogs that ran in and gave chase, often disturbing much of the game in the vicinity so that the shoot was spoiled. Dogs that whined, or even barked. Dogs that were tethered to their so-called 'masters" shooting sticks, until the dogs uprooted them and some unfortunates were brought to earth.

Many times, after seeing these wild dogs and having listened to their owners shouting at them in vain, have I had cause to wonder at the poor dog's background as far as basic training was concerned, and have been amazed at the total lack of understanding on the part of their owners. In these cases my sympathies have never been with the owners whose shooting was being spoilt, and whose money spent on their dogs was wasted, but with the dogs themselves. Either the dogs were not properly trained in the first place, or, if they had been, their owners just did not know them, or how to handle them.

In many cases these owners were fortunate enough to be in the financial position to enable them to join the best syndicate shoots, very often the guns they fired were most probably Purdeys, and I have no doubt that these same people took the most meticulous care of their firearms by ensuring that they were religiously well-oiled. I could only wish that they took anything like as much trouble with their gundogs. For myself, I would sooner know of fifty guns being misused than see one potentially good dog mishandled. In fairness, I am not suggesting that these owners were ever actively unkind to their dogs, nor that the dogs lacked for anything in the way of good kenneling and the best of food, and even affection of a sort. Obviously what they did not have was any kind of mutual understanding with their owners, and I have no hesitation in saying that any dog that lacks this can never be a completely happy dog.

In some instances, the owners may genuinely have lacked sufficient time to keep their dogs in working order. This brings me to one of the sayings I hear most often from dog owners: 'Of course, my dog would be much better if only I had the time.' Initially, when I hear this remark my mood is one of anger and intolerance which, in turn, changes to despair. How is it that so many otherwise sensible people can lack the commonsense to realise that if they do not have the necessary time they cannot have the sort of dogs that they desire? It is a sad but true fact that the majority of these people seem readily to join what I call the 'Well, he's good enough for me' brigade, which in itself is really total surrender. Or perhaps, even worse, they develop what is tantamount to a hate relationship with their dogs which is totally unjustified. Personally, I have little or no time for those who say they haven't the time to keep their dogs right. Such people don't deserve to own dogs and they never will. Neither do I think it worth wasting one's breath on the 'good enough for me' lot because they will never have good dogs either.

Nor yet do I favour the 'wishful thinking' view of some owners whose gundogs habitually commit various misdemeanours and who fondly think that, given time, their dogs will 'come right'. If this were the case most professional trainers would be looking for another job because their services would seldom be required. Very few dogs just come right, because nearly all of them need the guidance and application of intelligent and thoughtful trainers who are prepared to correct errors before they become habitual.

For the uninitiated, let me explain that trainers can be placed into three separate categories; the amateurs, private professional trainers, and public professional trainers. Let me make it clear at the outset that at no time will I be attempting to disparage any of these three categories in relation to each other, but I will try to make some comparisons between what I can best describe as their general approach to training. Although I myself am a member of the last mentioned group, the public professionals, I would hasten to add that there are many amateur trainers and handlers whose well deserved successes at field trials I would have been proud to emulate.

In the main, it should be obvious that the amateurs are people who keep comparatively few dogs and train them as shooting dogs or for field trials, and that they generally do this as their hobby, without serious thought of financial gain. It follows that some of these people, being well-endowed financially, can afford to discard several unpromising dogs until they find one that suits their requirements. There are some amongst the amateur ranks whose undoubted skills at the job have been well and truly proven, whilst at the other

16

Page 17 (*above*) Be enthusiastic! Author, Maurice Hopper, shows how; (*below*) Curious to learn, anxious to please—the looks that tell character in early training

Page 18 (*left*) Get together! At heel, the lead held correctly for training; (*right*) At heel, the lead held incorrectly

end of the scale there are those who have a lot to learn, to say the least.

For obvious financial reasons there are not very many private professional trainers in the country, but I think they could be fairly described as the elite among the professionals. Obviously they have been engaged for their skill at producing extremely well-trained dogs for field trials and for everyday shooting, and their outstanding abilities are repeatedly in evidence when the rest of us compete with them at trials. But whilst I would be the last to attempt to try and minimise the obvious talents of these men, like some of the amateurs, they are often in a somewhat enviable position as regards producing well-trained dogs is concerned. If one is in the fortunate position of having almost un-limited shooting ground on which to train one's dogs, have comparatively few dogs to train and are able to dis-card those that are unsuitable, if one possesses real skill, and spends the necessary time at the pick of one's pupils, it is a foregone conclusion that a good trainer is bound to bring out some outstandingly good gundogs.

Clearly, it would be crass hypocrisy on my part were I to attempt to deny some envy of the position in which some of the best amateurs and the private professionals find themselves. Nor would I be doing them anything like justice were I to attempt to suggest that they pro-duced well-trained dogs brought out by easy methods, because I do not think good dogs are ever produced so easily.

But what of us, the public professionals? I can best describe our job by comparing it with that of the profes-sional boxer who learns his trade the hard way, by taking on all-comers in a boxing booth. Like the boxers, we need to learn to take a lot of hard knocks and to be resilient. Throughout his career a public professional trains and handles anything from fifty to a hundred dogs as compared to the other trainer's one. And so his knowledge of dogs' temperaments should be proportionately greater by comparison. At the same time he should also be intelligent enough to have acquired a sense of humility that is commensurate with his experience, because he should have learned how much he has yet to learn, since each pupil is so different that every one is an education in itself.

There must be many reasons why people do not take up professional gundog training as a career, and why fewer still stay the course at the job. We have no union, but the pay is poor in relation to the hours and work and the problems entailed. When I say it is a seven-day week job I mean just that, because, like the famous Windmill Theatre, whose motto was 'We never closed', we gundog trainers are forever on call. Indeed, when I say that a prospective client has knocked on my door at 11 pm on a Sunday night, my meaning will be clear. Why then does a man undertake such a career? I think the answer is clear—because of an overriding love of the job. Like a good schoolmaster whose aim is to bring out the best in each pupil, a good trainer is forever eager to gain an intimate understanding with each of his dogs and to bring out the best in them. To do this the trainer must know himself and be master of himself because, if he is not, he can never be master of his dogs.

When I accept a client's spaniel for training the average period the dog remains with me is for five or six months and I have learnt from hard won experience that this time goes rapidly. A professional must learn to judge his pupil intimately as an individual and he cannot afford a major mistake. If, at any time, he is over-severe with a sensitive dog, or alternatively, too soft with a bold one, he must pay very dearly for his mistakes, for he will find he is weeks behind in his training schedule.

Ideally a trainer needs more qualities than any of us poor mortals possess, but I would say that a true love of dogs is essential; not, I would stress, the sloppy, sentimental version of those who mistakenly stuff their pet poodles with sweets, but the love that means a desire to reach a true understanding with each of one's trainees. I have tried to make a list of some of the qualities that the ideal trainer might possess, and since this list is multifarious I decided to go through the alphabet:

| | |
|---|---|
| A | Adaptability, alertness, authority |
| B | Big-heartedness |
| C | Commonsense, concentration |
| D | Determination |
| E | Endeavour, endurance, enthusiasm |
| F | Friendship |
| G | Good humour |
| H | Honesty, humility |
| I | Imagination, insight, intuition, interest |
| J | Justice |
| K | Kindliness, knowledge |
| L | Love, logic |
| M | Mastery |
| N | Naturalness |
| O | Observation |
| P | Patience, perception |
| Q | Quickness of decision |

| | |
|---|---|
| R | Rational thinking, resolution |
| S | Sense of humour, sensibility, sincerity, sympathy |
| T | Thoughtfulness |
| U | Understanding |
| V | Vision |
| W | Will-power |
| X? | Appreciation of the dogs we cannot fathom! |
| Y | Youthfulness of approach |
| Z | Zealousness |

There can hardly be one of us, myself least of all, who possesses all of these qualities in sufficiency and in the right proportion. Indeed, it is well that no one does, for he would need to be an almost perfect being, and therefore unbearable! Whilst most of these qualities are self-explanatory the apposition of some would need underlining. If I were to give priority it would definitely be to the As, the Cs and the Is.

No matter if he knows every sequence of the job of training spaniels, nor however long or wide his experience, a trainer should constantly be *adaptable*, and thus he needs to be *alert* to every contingency. I believe that all dogs are hypersensitive to a trainer's air of quiet *authority* and that his confidence, or lack of it, is immediately transmitted to his pupils.

If I were to be asked what is the most important attribute that any trainer can possess, the power of *concentration* would come very near the top of the list. Most trainers fail to appreciate the importance of this quality, for there are still far too many people who mistakenly imagine that prolonged sessions of so-called training, stretching for a period of 2-3 hours are equally, or even more, beneficial than a much briefer concentrated effort. If this were really the case it is certain that no professional trainer could possibly produce dogs that could compete favourably in competition in Field Trials, nor in the shooting field, with those that the best amateurs could bring out. For all professionals have at least from fifteen to twenty dogs to attend to at the same time and it is mathematically impossible for them to spend 2 hours a day training one dog only. It would be quite wrong for me to speak for every member of my profession because, like the dogs, we are all individuals and therefore different. But speaking for myself, I can only say that after I have had about three dogs out in succession on 15-minute training sessions I find that I am temporarily exhausted mentally with the concentrated effort, and that I need to get away from the job for a while and have a quiet smoke whilst I recharge the batteries: I will only add to this by stating that, apart from picking up at various shoots, the best dogs I have ever trained have never had more training than 15 minutes per day, five days a week on average, but each second of the time was concentrated effort. (There are obvious exceptions to this rule, as when everything goes wrong in training.) In short, 15 minutes of concentration should be more productive than 2 hours of woolgathering.

*Imagination* is something that could well cover a chapter under its own heading. I must not let my own imagination run away with me but I would like to give one personal aspect. Having watched many amateurs at work and having listened to them talking on the subject, I often feel that many are over-influenced by the statutory training as practised in training classes for dogs of all breeds. Whilst I will allow that basic obedience in a well-trained spaniel is a necessity, it requires a good deal more than this to control a spaniel who is, for the most part, a mobile dog whilst he is still in motion. In other words, one needs the control whilst the dog is still in motion and here one needs not only control, but imagination also. I shall deal with this in a later chapter.

*Insight,* too, is a quality that can be approached from many angles and could well occupy several pages on its own. It is the ability to be able to 'read' a dog accurately and to know what makes him tick. And, just as there are very few doctors and veterinary surgeons who are truly good diagnosticians, so also there are not many trainers who can easily 'read' the majority of dogs. The same applies to *sensitivity.* A truly sensitive person has a 'feeling' for a dog as an individual and he is thus able to give encouragement, or apply restraint, in the right proportion and at the right moment. Last, but by no means least I must include *sincerity,* for I believe that all dogs are highly sensitive as to what is genuine and what is phoney in man.

I often think the difference between many an amateur and an experienced professional is that, whereas the amateur is often liable to take his dog out to see just what the dog will do, the professional takes a dog out with a prearranged and predetermined idea of what the dog will do. This is obviously not so applicable to the very earliest stages of training but, once he is reasonably satisfied that he knows his pupil, this should be the attitude to the job in hand (with the proviso that he should always be adaptable to whatever circumstances may prevail). The trainer should also have learnt that any attempt to rush a dog into the excitements of the shooting field before it is really ready, is fraught with disaster, because he should already know that unless his pupil is almost pluperfect at home, without the excitements, he will never survive the temptations in the shooting field itself.

Sometimes when I talk to people about some of the complexities of training gundogs they look as mystified as I should were I placed in the cockpit of a modern aircraft, facing all the dials, knobs and buttons which confront the pilot of one of these big planes. Whilst it might seem at first that there can be no connection between the cockpit of an aircraft and the problems of gundog training, there is one similarity: if one does not know which button to press in an aircraft, and at exactly the precise moment, one is bound for disaster, and in many ways this is equally true of gundog training. But when I see a look of mystification or confusion in the face of my listener I naturally feel that I have failed in my duty as a teacher because my aim is to clarify rather than confuse. At the same time it would be quite wrong for me to try and pretend to the novice that gundog training and handling is a job which anyone can learn in six easy lessons, because this is not the case. And in these days where so many people seem to want potted versions of all sorts of subjects, which in turn must lead them to becoming jacks of all trades and masters of none, I must refuse to join those that pander to over-simplification, because were I to do so I should be doing a gross injustice, not only to my reader, but also to spaniels, a breed that I love. Thus, if one can accept the premise that there can be no absolute blue print for training, because of the variances of the individual, one can then consider the normal sequences of training, and these I will write about in due course.

And so it must surely amount to this. The trainer re
quires:

    (a) An intimate knowledge of the dog as ar
        individual.
    (b) A clear and positive understanding of trainin
        and handling, and the right sequence.
    (c) The positive and confident approach to the jol
        —to which all dogs are hypersensitive.

*Chapter 2*

# CHOOSING A PUPPY

It is of little use to try and persuade people to transfer their affections from one breed to another, for so often their first love is also their last. For instance, if the dog a man first owned was a Clumber, and it was a good one, the odds are that he will adhere to the breed for the future. But I am not writing this in an attempt to change the opinions of those who already have tried and trusted favourites of one particular breed, because my aim is to try and give the best sort of guidance to those who have not yet owned a spaniel, but are seeking a good one. There are still a great many people who do not realise that there are no less· than seven different breeds of spaniel as recognised by the Kennel Club. These are the Clumber, Cocker, English Springer, Field, Irish Water, Sussex and Welsh Springer. Which is the best?

Many people do not consider success at field trials as the be-all and end-all as far as assessing the merits of gundogs is concerned, and to a certain extent I would agree with them. I can appreciate that not everyone wants a dog to be quite as high-powered as some of the

27

best field trial dogs are. At the same time, just as motor-car rallies must surely give more than a useful guide as to the performance of different makes of car, so also must field trials be equally helpful in proving a breed's consistency.

For the uninitiated, certain facts should be made known about field trials for spaniels. Most of the spaniel societies hold two stakes at trials, the novice and the open, and in the open stake it is necessary to be placed first or second in order to qualify for the spaniel championship at the end of the season. At the championship the Cockers have their own stake which is exclusive to this breed. The other stake is open to the other six breeds of spaniel, and it must be a notable fact that since the last war no breed other than the English Springer has ever qualified for this stake. If greater proof of the superiority of the English Springer were needed I cannot think how else it could be proven.

I am aware that there are some really excellent shooting dogs to be found from amongst any of the other breeds of spaniel, or else they would not have their adherents. Looking back over the years I have seen a few Field Spaniels that were really outstanding workers, and indeed in the years between the wars that brilliant trainer Dick Male trained two Fields which became field trial champions. The Field Spaniel closely resembles the English Springer in all but colour, the majority being either all black or all liver. Sadly the number of Field Spaniels bred today is few. And how can one fairly assess the merits of the Cocker in comparison with the English Springer? I have many friends who train Cockers for field trials and I have seen many brilliant working spaniels amongst them, but not even their staunchest adherents would deny that many Cockers are far from easy to train. On more than one occasion I have seen Cockers running at field trials, competing on level terms with English Springers and the Cocker has been judged the winner. This in itself must surely prove that on their day the best Cockers are at least the equal of any other breed of spaniel. But having trained many Cockers myself, some good, some bad, I can claim some personal knowledge of the breed. I have also attended many trials where Cockers were running and I have also judged them. In my view, the best of them are brilliant, but I think there are still too many whose performances are inconsistent, for they are apt to be very good one day and very bad the next. Hence, it must follow that my choice is the same as many other trainers, the English Springer.

If I should seem to have made the choice of breed a comparatively simple matter I cannot say that I think the choice of an individual puppy is nearly as easy and the reasons for this are manifold.

Some years ago I wrote an article entitled, 'A Tailor-made Gundog', and this in itself needs some explanation, because the message I was trying to get across to my reader was that, ideally, the dog should be suited to his handler temperamentally. There is no doubt in my mind that there are certain trainers who are best suited to train and handle the bolder type of dog, whilst there are others who are capable of bringing out the best in the most sensitive type. Speaking for myself, I have a definite preference for training and handling the latter type of dog, but at the same time I fully appreciate that not everyone shares this preference.

29

There is all the difference in the world between the dog, or puppy, that is just soft and the puppy that is basically sensitive (or shy, if you wish) but also possesses real courage, providing that it is brought out by careful and thoughtful handling. To put it tritely, the soft dog will always be soft because there is no basic courage to develop, but it does require some perception to assess the difference, particularly in puppyhood. Obviously the bold type of puppy, being a complete extrovert, is not difficult to judge, but if one is to dismiss the others summarily, I think one could easily pass by some potentially great gundogs. The reason I stress this is because some of the best gundogs I have ever trained were extremely shy as puppies. It should be plain that these need much care and patience if their trainers are to bring out the best in them, but for my part I have always found it very rewarding whenever I have been able to win over a shy dog. One of the reasons for this is that they are always so patently grateful for the understanding treatment they have received, and consequently they tend to be more eager to please.

However, one point on which I think the majority are agreed is that the influence of the dam is greater than that of the sire on the progeny, and if this is the case it is vital for the prospective puppy owner to be very careful in his selection of the bitch. I do not think that it is anything like sufficient to attempt to make an assessment of a working spaniel on just one viewing. I think that consistency should be the criterion, which means that the prospective dam should prove her abilities over a period of time.

As anyone who has bred and reared a litter of puppies already knows they can be expensive, especially if the

30

litter is large, and for this reason most breeders prefer to sell their puppies at from eight to ten weeks old. Undoubtedly, it is a far easier matter to judge a puppy's potential at six months of age, but comparatively few breeders can afford to run them on until this age. Whilst I would never claim anything like infallibility in selecting the right puppy, especially at the tender age of eight or nine weeks, in order to help the novice I must try and offer some useful advice and so I should like to introduce an imaginary litter.

When I first go to see a litter of youngsters I like to look at them for a time as they play naturally, in an uninhibited way, in their pen, so that I can observe their actions and watch their general behaviour, and after I have had a good look at them I generally ask the breeder if I can have them out individually. For the purpose of demonstration let us assume that there are seven puppies from which to choose.

I had already noted as the puppies played in their pen that four of them were plainly bold, of a naturally friendly type and were eager for closer acquaintance, whilst the other three tended to keep their distance. But even before I had any of them out of the pen one of the bold puppies failed to attract me because I judged his eye to be hard and, rightly or wrongly, hard-eyed dogs have never appealed to me as I have generally found them to be hard-headed too. The eyes are the first thing I look at in any puppy and what I like to find is the expression that is at once alert, intelligent and kind.

Next I picked up one of the other bold puppies and took him out of the pen, carrying him several yards away so that he would not be distracted by the others.

31

Although, throughout a dog's training I only ask them to fetch and carry dummies etc, whose outer core is of soft material, at this tender age of eight weeks it can do no harm to introduce them to the fascination of a half-empty matchbox. Just as babies are attracted to a rattle, so most puppies are intrigued by the sound of a shaken matchbox. At first, this puppy did not show much interest in the matchbox but after I had rattled it a few times his tail began to wag and, when I had his full attention, I threw it some 8 feet away on to the close cropped lawn. He ran to it and sniffed it but made no attempt to pick it up. I went and fetched it myself and gave him another try. This time he ran to it and picked it up, but then he ran away with it, shook it and then dropped it and failed to show any further interest. After this I returned him to his pen and brought out another one to try. I did not have very much success with this puppy either because he showed little or no interest in the matchbox and seemed only to want to gallop around investigating everything else.

But the last of the bold puppies was different altogether. Immediately I rattled the box he showed a lively interest and when I threw it he ran and picked it up. When I gave a high-pitched whistle he moved towards me as I backed away, at the same time crouching as low as I could (I crouched because all youngsters seem to find one less formidable if one can decrease one's height to nearer their own level, as it seems to give them more confidence.) He delivered the box to me confidently, tail wagging merrily at the same time, and when I removed it from his mouth he released it unhesitatingly, thus showing a naturally tender mouth. After this, I just gave him two more retrieves which he did equally well, then I replaced him in the pen, deciding then and there to buy him if I could.

When I turned my attention to the three shy puppies one of them failed to interest me because her expression was sulky. I have never liked this type of temperament as they are rarely co-operative in training, so I did not take her from the pen.

It is not easy to describe why I took a liking to the next puppy, a bitch, even before I had her out of the pen, but I can only say that I had a feeling that she had a great potential. At first she was undoubtedly shy, but I took my time and did my best to make friends with her by stroking and fondling her and by talking to her quietly. When I showed her the matchbox she looked at it apprehensively to begin with, and when I gave it a gentle rattle she seemed even more doubtful, but after a short while she decided that it was unlikely to harm her and her tail began to wag with more momentum. When I threw the box she ran to it, gave it another brief examination and picked it up from the ground. At that moment I gave her a whistle and backed away, crouching once again. Her movement towards me was tentative but she regained her confidence and I was able to get her to deliver to hand. I praised her gently, muttering endearments at the same time. After this she did two more retrieves for me with more speed and increased enthusiasm and I knew then that I wanted to take this puppy home too.

I did not spend much time with the other shy puppy, not only because he seemed lethargic, but because I thought he was generally speaking a bit soft and lacked courage. So my choices were the best of the bold puppies and the shy bitch to which I was so attracted.

These two puppies not only appealed to me from the point of view of their performances and temperaments but also from their physical characteristics. They both bid fair to have dark eyes and I have always preferred dark-eyed dogs. They also had long necks set well on sloping shoulders and their chests were deep. Their forelegs were straight with good bone, whilst their tails were set low on well rounded hindquarters. Last, but not least, they both had proportionately broad heads and kindly, intelligent expressions. And while I would never suggest for one moment that all dogs with broad heads are intelligent, for we all know the allusion with regard to humans who are thick headed, at the same time I have never favoured the domed type head in spaniels which, unfortunately, is often found to be attractive to judges in the show ring. For what it is worth, all the really great field trial champions that I have ever seen had proportionately broad skulls and I feel that for this reason it should be counted as a very important physical attribute.

Lastly, a few words of advice about docking. Especially if one has field trials in view I would strongly advise against buying a puppy that has been docked short as this will deprive him of all his style. In general, more than half of the tail should be left when it is docked, as it is far better to be too long than too short.

After reviewing what I have just written about this imaginary litter I feel that I should underline the fact that this description is no more than a cameo. The point that I am trying to make is that no one can judge a dog's potential on just one viewing and it is more than probable that some of the puppies I rejected could well turn out to be excellent workers. But it is the same when one

Page 35 In training, a spaniel marks the dummy launcher

Page 36 Hup! The gundog handler's most useful word

is judging field trials, since one can only decide on what one sees on the day.

And in concluding this chapter it may sound trite to say that in choosing a puppy breeding will tell. On the whole, I should recommend the best field trial blood as I think that, generally speaking, this is where the best working blood is to be found. But it should be obvious that a working dog should be bred from several generations of working parents, and one should avoid at all costs those that come from stock that have been bred for the show ring only.

*Chapter 3*

# OF WHISTLES, WORDS OF COMMAND AND EQUIPMENT

Whatsoever one does throughout a dog's training, from the outset both care and forethought must have a profound bearing on his future behaviour and efficiency, and the longer one trains dogs the more one realises the consequences of these matters. Thus I would not dismiss lightly the importance of the equipment used in an attempt to produce a really efficient gundog, since everything one does has its own effect for good or ill in one's ultimate objective. For just as a first class tennis player would be unsatisfied with a poorly strung racquet, or a concert violinist with a second rate violin, no good dog trainer should make use of unsuitable equipment.

Some people seem to think that a dog's lead is not of any particular importance, but I would disagree entirely. I am not thinking particularly of the quality of the lead, although it naturally needs to be strong, but of its length, as too short a lead is quite useless for gaining the necessary control. And, since I must confess that during the years that I have been training I have mislaid countless dog leads, for reasons of economy I now make my own leads. I use an ordinary rope clothes line, such as can be purchased at any ironmongers, and cut it to suitable lengths of not less than 5 feet, thus allowing for tying a comfortable hand loop some 8 inches long. I then tie the other end to a choke chain. For general use with the average-sized spaniel I like a choke chain 2 feet long (this length is obviously taken before the chain has been passed through its ring in the proper manner) preferably one with a fine mesh, providing it is strong, as I think it gives one greater control. As for the purpose and value of a lead of the correct length I will write about this in the following chapter, when describing the actual lead training.

There are many people also who give little thought to the sort of dummies they use, but if the right lead is important so also are the dummies. For the average trainer I think that several dummies are necessities and that these should be of varying weights and circumferences. The weights of the dummies that I use vary from approximately 5oz for the smallest to some $2\frac{1}{2}$lb for the largest, and for general purposes I use dummies of about $1\frac{1}{2}$lb. The circumference of these varies from $7\frac{1}{2}$ inches for the smallest to 13 inches for the largest. The reason that I have such a supply of dummies for different dogs at certain stages of their training is again something I will write about later. I think it is also necessary to give some thought and care as to how the dummies are made. And, whilst I will not be specific as to the material used as an outer covering, although there is much to be said for canvas for its strength, the main point to emphasise is that the centre core of wood, which I employ as a makeweight, must be completely cushioned so that there are no hard edges for the dog to feel when he retrieves. Any hard substance tends to promote a hard mouth.

In making the heavier dummies I generally cut a short length of wood about 8 inches long, of an appropriate weight, and use this as the core. In order to cushion this I use foam rubber, both for its pliability and for the ease with which it can be cut suitably to the dimensions required. The average length of the larger dummies is one foot. When I enclose it in its outer covering, be it a stocking or canvas, I try to ensure that there are no loose ends for a dog to catch hold of as these tend to make them sloppy retrievers, whilst well-balanced, well-made dummies teach them to carry in an evenly balanced manner. When making the smallest dummy, I do not use anything for makeweight, simply squeezing the foam rubber into a small stocking and then tying or stitching the open end.

I must also include here what is generally known as the American dummy thrower, with its appropriate dummy. Like many others I have found this an invaluable piece of equipment since it can be fired at varying distances of 100 yards and over, and its uses are many, as I shall describe in due course.

With regard to whistles, for the moment let it suffice to say that I use only two types of whistle. One of these is the Staghorn whistle, which I blow to recall a dog when he is retrieving. To be more precise, I give him a double blast on this whistle, simultaneous with his pick up of the retrieve, and this has the double effect of hastening both the actual pick-up and also his return. The other whistle, which I regard as by far the most important, is the Acme Silent whistle. Like many other trainers and handlers I value it highly both for its obvious quietness together with its extraordinary effectiveness at all ranges, which is the result of its very high-pitched tone. Briefly, I give one long blast on this whistle to stop a spaniel, and two short blasts to turn him when he is hunting.

I do not think that there can be anything connected with training that requires more thoughtful consideration than the words of command. In order to illustrate this let me recall two cases where thoughtless use of words caused not only great confusion to the dogs concerned but near ruination for the purposes for which they were being trained. In the first place I am telling a tale against myself, for I was the culprit here. In this instance the dog was a collie and the incident occurred over thirty years ago when I was on the staff of the War Dogs Training School. For a time this collie seemed to be progressing very nicely as a messenger dog for which I was training him, until he suddenly developed the habit of barking when he was despatched, a cardinal sin for a messenger dog. I was utterly perplexed as to the reason for his developing this habit and I am quite certain that I would never have fathomed the cause of it on my own. Fortunately, I had the benefit of the opinion of a friend, Bill Adams, a far better trainer than myself, who was able to pinpoint the cause. The standard word of command to despatch a messenger dog was 'Get on' and the mistake I made was that when I exercised Sandy during his play period I used to tell him to 'Have a run'. Although these words might not at first appear too similar, they were close enough to confuse the dog, so that he did not differentiate between play time and the duty period. Thus he developed the habit of playing and barking at the wrong time.

The other case occurred some two years ago and this time the dog was a working spaniel. His owner and trainer is a high-ranking soldier who had already trained some more than useful gundogs, but this spaniel had developed a very bad habit which he could not account for. The bitch would retrieve to within one yard of her owner, then she would stop and drop her retrieve. When I saw her in action I was soon able to tell why this was happening. Her handler was in the habit of telling her to 'Bring it on up' when she was retrieving, and, since the traditional word of command for stopping a spaniel is the word 'Hup', I pointed this out to the gentleman that he was virtually saying to his bitch 'Bring it on—Sit'. This caused her to sit before she reached him, thus resulting in the confusion and spoiling the retrieve.

I hope these two illustrations of errors made will help to demonstrate the importance of dissimilarity between words of command. Although I realise that each trainer has his own favourite orders I give below a list of those I use:

| Hup | when ordering to sit or stop |
| Heel | ,, ,, ,, walk at heel |
| Fetch It | ,, ,, ,, retrieve |
| Gently | ,, ,, ,, release retrieve |
| Back *or* | |
| Come On | ,, ,, ,, come |
| Seek On | ,, ,, ,, start hunting |
| Over | ,, ,, ,, jump |
| Hi-lost | ,, ,, ,, hunt for a lost bird |
| Get Out | ,, ,, ,, hunt further out |
| No | when ordering *not* to do anything |

To these I should add the order 'Quiet'. used not only when a dog is noisy in kennel but also out shooting, if there is any tendency to whine. And once again, I will underline the dissimilarity in sound among these orders, which means that the dogs will learn to associate each different sound with the appropriate action.

I do not think that it is anything like sufficient just to know a suitable list of words of command because the tone in which they are given is vital since, as I have already stressed, all dogs are impressed by the conviction, or lack of it, which lies behind the orders they are given. They are certainly not impressed if the volume of sound is unnecessarily loud since they can unerringly detect the lack of confidence in their handlers. Anyone who has served in the army knows that the officer who gives his orders in a tone of firm but quiet authority commands more than twice the respect when compared with the loud-mouthed blusterer, and it is exactly the same sort of thing in the case of a handler and his dog. Although I must own there are times when I am as guilty as the next man in the matter of being too noisy when handling, I know that the best dogs I have trained and handled have been those that I have been able to work with the minimum of noise. When one goes around the country to attend various shoots, and even some field trials, one cannot fail to notice that the standard of handling is very often extremely low, and I am referring particularly to unnecessary noisiness. And whilst every field trial judge has his own particular phobia, my own is unnecessary noise, and this is naturally underlined by those comparatively few handlers who still attain the best results by quiet, authoritative handling. Indeed I have often wished that some dogs could have carried tape recorders on their backs and that they could have played back to their handlers the absolute gibberish they heard, purporting to be orders. In many cases it would have made about as much sense as an Indian merchant berating a Chinese mendicant!

## Chapter 4

# EARLY TRAINING—PART ONE

First let me say that there can be no blueprint for training because of the dissimilarities between each of the puppies. Indeed, I think that the only puppy for which one could produce a blueprint is the perfect puppy, and he or she just does not exist. Amongst all the spaniels that I have ever trained I think that only one ever came really close to this standard and if ever there was misunderstanding between us I should judge that the errors were undoubtedly mine.

To begin with one should consider, in the broadest sense, just what a spaniel is required to do. On this basis he is needed to hunt and find, and also to retrieve. If one is agreed that these are his basic functions, it is surely logical that the primary instinct is to hunt, and it must follow that retrieving is a secondary thought to the average spaniel. Therefore, I think it vital to make them really reliable retrievers before they know about the joy of hunting. If one does not tackle the job in this sequence, most spaniels will hunt but will ignore the retrieving and leave this to their handlers. Hence one should make every endeavour to make each puppy into a thoroughly reliable retriever before he sees or hunts for game of any kind. But before I say anything about the primary lessons in spaniel training I should like to discuss the age to start.

Up to a certain age there is no doubt that this can be an elastic thing for I know that some trainers give their puppies elementary lessons even as early as at nine or ten weeks. I would certainly not dispute the wisdom of this, not only because it is something that I have never attempted, but because I know that some of those trainers who have started this early have been experts whose wisdom I would not have the temerity to question. But since I can only write on the basis of my own experience let me say that I do not normally commence a spaniel's training until he is six months old. I think it is doubtful whether the average spaniel puppy is ready to absorb much serious training before this age and that it is probably just as well to allow him to enjoy his puppyhood until then. Whenever I accept a client's spaniel for training I prefer to take him at six months of age and then, if he knows no more than his name, it means that I have a clean sheet on which to start. At the same time I should stress that I do not care to take them much later than this since they seem to learn many bad habits if they are not taken in hand about this time.

Obviously I cannot speak for every trainer, but if I were asked what are the two biggest problems that I generally have to contend with in spaniel training I should unhesitatingly say retrieving and quartering. I will readily agree that with some spaniels neither of these is much of a problem since some are almost perfect natural retrievers, and some seem to quarter their ground with the minimum of guidance. In these cases the job is made very easy for the trainers. But there are many more that are reluctant retrievers, or just bad retrievers, and there are many that need intense and prolonged training in order to teach them to quarter.

Before going into details about the earliest lessons in retrieving I should like to say something about the best sort of venue, and the best conditions, for these lessons to take place. The first and most obvious vital necessity is that the training ground must be somewhere where one can be certain of being entirely alone with the puppy and where there are no distractions of any kind, but I do not think that even this is quite enough. I am a great believer in selecting a place for early training where the conditions, and the terrain, are an aid to the job in hand, and here I am thinking of the early retrieving lessons in particular. Were I in the fortunate position of having every possible facility for training I think that I should even go so far as to erect what I can call a 'training lane', as an aid to teaching young dogs to retrieve. The idea for this occurred to me when I remembered what I used to call the 'nursery lane' for messenger dogs at the War Dogs Training School during the last war. This was simply a straight lane, about 8 feet wide, built of posts and wire netting 6 feet high. It was erected on short cut turf and was, as far as I can recollect, some 50 yards long. The lane was fully enclosed with an entrance gate at one end and, although one would not require this length for teaching puppies to retrieve, it seems to me it would be ideal for young-sters since it would not allow them to take any diversions. Since I do not have this facility I make use of the nearest place to this and here I am fortunate in that my cottage is situated down a narrow lane which is rarely

47

frequented. It also has the necessary natural advantages as the hedges are thick, so that the chances of a puppy diverting with a retrieve are very limited.

In describing the early training as far as is possible I want to take my reader along with me with a six month old puppy from the very outset, from the moment I first take him from his kennel, assuming he knows nothing more than his name. When I first take him out I put him on the choke chain, holding the lead at its fullest length. The pattern never seems to vary since nearly every puppy starts by 'fighting' the lead which I purposely allow him to do. If he drags back and loiters behind then I tug him until he finds that it is far less uncomfortable if he moves with me. Or, if he pulls forward or sideways, he is soon apt to learn that tightening the choke chain is not at all comfortable either. And so at this very early stage I do not attempt to give him lead training in the real sense but allow him to learn for himself the power of the lead and the choke chain. However, throughout this book I will make no apologies if I state repeatedly that there are exceptions to every rule because of individual temperaments, and if I have a puppy that hangs back from acute shyness I think it is vital to give him every encouragement by bending down to pat him, and by trying to gain his confidence by every means possible. By the time we have progressed some hundred yards from the kennels, however stumblingly, both I and the puppy will be somewhat out of breath. I then allow several minutes to pass so that we can both get our breaths back and become more composed for this first attempt at retrieving.

Many amateurs teach their puppies to sit before giving them their first retrieving lessons. Although I do not think that this is the right sequence in training, the real mistake is to insist on the puppies being in the sitting position when given their first retrieving lessons, with the net result that a great many puppies become 'sticky' when asked to go for their retrieves. When I take a puppy out for his first retrieving lessons I give him every possible encouragement to 'run in' to the retrieve and I make every effort to keep him happy, so that he will come to regard these first lessons as something enjoyable, as opposed to being restrictive. The more restrictive obedience lessons will come a little later.

Now let me return to the point where I and my puppy had arrived at the chosen place in the lane for the first attempts at retrieving, and we will assume that we have both recovered our breaths after our 'battle' with the lead. For this first lesson I invariably use a tennis ball as I cannot think of anything more tempting than a rolling ball and, however trite it may sound, all that I am attempting to do here is first to capture the puppy's attention and interest in the ball, then to entice him to go and pick it up and bring it back to me. I kneel beside him and, holding him lightly round the neck, show him the ball and let him sniff it and inspect it thoroughly. Once I have done this and I have his full attention, I roll the ball down the lane releasing him simultaneously. Each time I despatch the puppy I give him his first order 'Fetch it', so that he will learn to associate this with the act of retrieving. When I first roll the ball there are about six, or seven, different things that can happen: 1 The puppy can remain where he is, making no attempt to go after it. 2 He may run to it and then show no interest in picking it up. 3 He

49

may pick it up and run in the opposite direction. 4 He may pick it up and diverge to right or left. 5 He may bring it so far towards me and drop it. 6 He may bring it towards me and try to bolt past. 7 He may deliver it perfectly to hand. Although I am long past the stage where I get despondent if the initial attempts prove fruitless, the puppies that would give me most concern are those in the categories 1 and 2, and before giving an account of my actions with the puppies that are natural retrievers I should like to write first about the problem puppies.

It should be obvious that the first thing one must try to do is to gain the puppy's interest in the tennis ball and in an attempt to achieve this I try rolling, or bouncing the ball. In the majority of cases this does at least tempt the puppy to run after it and investigate, even if he does not pick it up. I will not be specific as to how many attempts I may make with those puppies that show a total lack of interest in the tennis ball, or with those that consistently refuse to pick it up, but if I find that after a few days I am still making no headway it is almost a certainty that the only remedy with these puppies is to resort to force retrieving which I describe in another chapter.

Although the last thing I wish to do is to deter, or to confuse the novice by over-complicating matters let me say that there are certain puppies whose behaviour can baffle even the most experienced professionals. I do not want to be so uncharitable as to suggest that these puppies are necessarily mentally deficient but in modern parlance I think that their human counterparts would be classified as 'mixed-up kids'. These are the puppies whose behaviour indicates at one moment that they are semi-shy, at another that they are semi-playful, at another they are cunning, even at times hard-headed and at others just sulky, which is probably the greatest barrier of all. In these cases it would not only be foolish of me to attempt to describe how to deal with this type of puppy but it would also be hypocritical, for as they are utterly unpredictable, I do not know the answer, and if one does not know the answer one will never train the dog. There may well be those who disagree with me but personally I do not think that this type of puppy is worth wasting one's time on and that the best thing to do is to give him away to a good home as a pet, and then start training another one. If it is of any comfort I have found that this sort of puppy is rare.

But some of the other problem puppies are more than worth taking the trouble to sort out and, speaking professionally again, I regard these as a challenge. If such puppies are trained and handled properly many of them should turn out first-class gundogs, but once again it must depend to a very large extent on the trainer's ability to analyse correctly the reason for each puppy's behaviour. Does he react in whatever way he does react because of playfulness, hard-headedness, cunning or shyness? Once one is able to satisfy oneself that one knows these answers one should then know how best to deal with each individual problem.

Whatever the problem may be I am not going to be so foolish as to try to suggest the basic cause but in one or two cases I can possibly generalise and after this it must be left to each trainer to make his own assessments. For instance, the puppy that picks up the ball and then runs away with it in the opposite direction is often doing so because of playfulness, and it is up to the trainer to use his intelligence in order to overcome this ploy. This frequently is a case of trial and error. Personally, if I have one of these puppies that consistently tries to run in the opposite direction with his retrieves I generally take him into my dog yard and test him out within its confines. This is a yard some 15 yards in length and 5 yards wide and since the railings are 6 feet high he is unable to divert nor to run off with his retrieves. More often than not I am successful in urging these puppies to deliver their retrieves under these conditions, and sometimes it has proved sufficient so that they co-operate once I try them outside again. But most puppies are not foolish and sometimes they get up to their old tricks once they see that there are no barriers to defeat their playfulness. Once again it may well be a matter of having to resort to force retrieving. As for those puppies that divert to right or left with their retrieves, the immense value of my lane, with its thick hedges, will immediately be apparent and I can only suggest that trainers with these problems should seek out a place where the conditions are similar.

The next point I find difficult to describe but I must make the attempt since I consider it to be of vital importance. I am referring here to the matter of timing. This is something that one can only learn from practice and experience, but it is of very great importance in handling a gundog throughout his career. My first reference to this will be in relation to handling the 'reluctant deliverer' and the point about the necessity of one's sense of timing here is something I will refer to presently.

If I think that with certain puppies I can best obtain my objective of urging them to deliver by lying down

Page 53 The pick-up—unhesitating, deliberate, but quick

Page 54 Correct delivery—the retrieve held until the trainer is
ready to receive

on my back I am only too willing to do so. For this reason I generally wear clothes that are best suited for lying down in dust, or even mud if necessary, and for these purposes I would recommend an anorak and waterproof leggings as the most suitable attire. I have often found it effective to lie prone in order to tempt shy puppies to deliver for they are more willing to approach at this level.

I referred previously to the importance of correct timing in relation to training and this will first be put to the test in these early retrieving lessons. The exact moment when one should recall the puppy with his retrieve is simultaneous with the pick-up, and I have often found to my cost that if I am as much as a second too early with the recall, or a second too late, this has proved sufficient to ruin the retrieve. If I have called too soon it has often resulted in the puppy leaving the retrieve, and if it has been late it may have meant that he tended to divert, or play. As for the recall itself in these early stages I do not intend to be at all specific as to my words or actions because they vary with each individual puppy. In some cases a high pitched call of 'good little dog', brings the best results, whilst with the bolder and more playful ones a much deeper tone of command such as 'Come on' is often more effective. As far as my actions are concerned, in the majority of cases I turn and trot away simultaneous with the pick-up, giving the recall sound at the very same time. When the puppy gets near to me as I retreat I turn and crouch, trying to urge him to deliver to hand.

I will not be precise as to exactly how long I can afford to tolerate the puppy that persistently drops his retrieves before delivering but clearly one dare not allow this to become habitual. If I find after three weeks or so that he still persists in doing so then it is plain that something must be done to correct this. The puppy must be taught to hold his retrieve and not to release it until he is ordered to do so. My usual method is to take him out on the lead and, once we are well away from the kennels, I make him sit and then, when I have his full attention, I open his mouth and place the dummy between his jaws and I close them over it gently. At the very same moment I give him the order 'Tight' which is the word that I want him to associate with the act of holding. I need hardly add that in the majority of cases the puppy will persist in dropping it almost immediately. It is a job that requires not only patience but also persistence on the part of the trainer and each time that the puppy drops the dummy one should pop it back, giving the order 'Tight' at the same moment, until one is successful in getting him to hold it for at least half a minute. Once he has done so he should be praised by stroking him gently and by telling him he is a 'Good dog'. When I am confident that he understands this order I take him out on the lead and after placing the dummy in his mouth I give the order 'Tight' and then I take him for a short walk, with him holding the dummy, and I repeat the quiet order 'Tight' as we walk along. If he holds it for two or three minutes I bend down and remove the dummy from his mouth to the order 'Gently'.

Assuming that we have progressed this far satisfactorily the next time we go out I make him sit again and I place the dummy in his mouth and order 'Tight'. Then I walk away some 15 yards and, if he is still holding the dummy, I order 'Back' which is my order to come. As he moves towards me I keep repeating 'Tight' and if he hangs on to the dummy until I remove it, saying 'Gently', I praise him again in a similar manner. Finally, if he has maintained this standard of performance when we go out on our next training session I make him sit again. I throw the dummy and, after a minute's interval, tell him to 'Fetch it'. When he turns towards me I give the order 'Tight' as he approaches and if he holds the dummy until I remove it I praise him once again. I need hardly add that I would expect this gradual progress to stretch over two or three weeks and that I would not dare to risk spoiling the final outcome by attempting to rush things.

## Chapter 5

# EARLY TRAINING—PART TWO

I should now like to write about the sequence of training in the early days with those puppies that are reliable natural retrievers. Any trainer, amateur or professional, should be thankful if he has a puppy that is a natural retriever, eager to pick up and deliver to hand, but I think it is of vital importance that he should give much thought and care as to the acceptance of the retrieve or else this can be ruined. But before I go into details I should like to recapitulate on the points that I made earlier about the sequence of training from the very outset.

If the puppy has proved that he will retrieve the tennis ball consistently I switch from the ball to the light dummy. I encourage him to run in to each retrieve at this stage and order 'Fetch it' each time I throw the dummy. All that I am trying to do is to get him to associate this order with the act of picking up and retrieving to hand. I try to keep up this training daily and I like him to do five good retrieves each day, no more no less. I think that if one attempts to do more than this he will probably become bored which could soon develop into his becoming a sloppy, inconsistent retriever.

At this stage I normally adopt the kneeling position for acceptance of the retrieve but the really important point that I should like to stress is that one should try at all costs to avoid the temptation to snatch the dummy. Naturally each puppy will vary in his or her approach, some tentatively, some perhaps a little over-enthusiastically, but in each case he should be encouraged to hold on to the dummy for at least half a minute until one removes it, saying 'Gently'. Each puppy will vary again in the strength of his hold, some having a light hold whilst others may be over-firm. In either case one should never pull the dummy away but ease it gently from the mouth as if it were very delicate and precious. With the puppy that seems reluctant to give it up I generally apply a little pressure of the lips on to the eye teeth and, should this not prove sufficient to make him release, then I will apply light pressure on his toes with my foot. I should add that I praise the puppy each time for a good delivery and especially at the end of each brief training session before I take him back to his kennel. If the puppy has done five retrieves a day, delivering consistently to hand, after a little over a fortnight I reckon that he has a clear understanding of his first order 'Fetch it' and that he is ready for the second stage of his early training.

The next thing I like to teach my puppy is his first lesson in obedience, sitting and staying. Providing that I have a puppy of average intelligence I have never found much difficulty in teaching him this lesson but I count the manner in which it is done of great importance. After leading the puppy well away from the kennels to a place where we can be assured of no distractions I am ready to give him his first obedience lesson. Still keeping him on the lead I press his buttocks to the ground and order 'Hup' at the same moment, since this is the command for sitting and staying. At first, of course, he will keep on getting up but one must persist until one is successful in getting him to remain seated for about a minute. I always raise my right hand, palm towards him, when he sits as I want him to learn to associate this sign with the action. Once I have succeeded in getting him to sit for a minute I bend down and praise him and then I take him back to his kennel.

For the next two or three days I will keep the lead on him when we go out for these lessons but I back away from him a little further each day, 3 yards, 5 yards and then perhaps 10 yards, leaving him in the sitting position for at least a minute. Should he get up and come towards me before the time is up I simply take him back again and persist until I have succeeded. The point that I should like to stress throughout these lessons is that once the puppy has remained seated for the required time I do not call him to me but I walk back to him each time and praise him in the sitting position. By adopting this practice he will learn that he is being praised for having remained sitting, which is the whole object of this exercise.

If all has gone well up to this point I will probably remove the lead from my puppy after ordering him to 'Hup' and then I back away about 15 yards or so if he still remains. In a day or two after this I could reasonably expect him to stay steady while I walk away and I increase the time and distance very gradually each time. And I will repeat that if he does move towards me I take him back to the very same position and I insist on his remaining there for the necessary time until I have succeeded.

I am very much averse to suggesting any particular time limit with regard to any aspect of gundog training, not only because the race is not always to the swift but because this is contrary to all the right concepts of training. However, as a matter of interest, I have usually found that if I have been training a puppy of average intelligence, and have kept up this gradual obedience training daily, that he has learnt to sit and stay for about 4 minutes at a distance of 70 yards, in about a fortnight, and this is my normal target.

The main point that I should like to underline in these early obedience lessons is the importance of giving the puppy one's total concentration. Since a dog is hypersensitive to this, it is really vital now because the impression that the puppy gets of his master's capabilities at this stage is likely to remain with him throughout his training career. The order 'Hup' should be given in a tone of firm, but quiet authority and the trainer's thoughts should never wander from the job in hand.

If the early training has been well-ingrained the puppy should have a clear understanding by now of two words of command—'Fetch it' and 'Hup'—and now is the time to marry the two together. In other words he must fetch, but not until he is ordered to do so. This is the first real test of steadiness. To start with I take him out on the lead again, and once we have reached a place where we can be assured of quietude and no distractions we should be ready to start this next lesson. Usually I do this training in my quiet lane in the earliest

61

stages, but in any case I would always choose some-where where the ground is open and where the puppy can see the dummy when it is thrown. With the puppy on the choke chain and holding the lead at its full length, I order 'Hup' firmly but quietly before I throw the dummy. Almost invariably he will attempt to 'run in' as I throw but, having a firm hold of the lead, I am able to check him and make him sit once again. After an interval of at least a minute I remove the lead and order 'Fetch it'. When he has delivered I put him back on the lead and go through a similar procedure. I only give him five retrieves a day and at this stage I expect him to make the attempt to run in, but having a hold of the lead I am in control and, as he moves when I throw, I step in front of him and repeat the order 'Hup'. After two or three days I would expect to be able to drop the lead on the ground and after telling him to 'Hup' I am ready to intercept if he moves when I throw the dummy.

Providing that all has gone well up to this point my next move is to remove the lead and choke chain and, after making him sit, I throw the dummy, always stand-ing in front of him when I throw so that I can intercept. After this it is simply a matter of gradual progress as I 'read' my puppy's increasing steadiness until I am able to stand beside him as I throw the dummy and then, when he is really steady, I stay behind him. Remember that this should be a gradual advancement, as in all training, and one should not be tempted to cut any corners by trying too much too soon.

If the puppy has proved his steadiness and has been retrieving to hand consistently for about three weeks or so, my next move would be to test him for hunting for the thrown dummy in light cover, such as tussocky grass. The main thing to remember here is that in the early stages of training a puppy nothing succeeds like success and therefore I would not only choose the lightest cover but I would also ensure when I cast the dummy that it was palpably obvious.

It is certainly very gratifying if the puppy has proved that he will retrieve the dummy consistently but the real test must come when he is asked to retrieve feather. Many shooting men state that they have the greatest difficulty in getting their gundogs to retrieve wood-cock, but, personally speaking, I have usually found that pigeons are the acid test. This is due, of course, to the loose feathers that cling so easily to their mouths and for this reason I would never dream of attempting to start a puppy on a freshly shot pigeon, but I would choose a cold one as the feathers are not so loose.

Some two years ago I gave a talk on spaniel training to some gamekeepers. After the talk we got together and one of the subjects we talked about was the retriev-ing of pigeons. I think I learnt a very useful tip that day. One of the keepers told me that he always started his youngsters off by placing the pigeon in a lady's nylon stocking, cut to the appropriate length. I have tried this since then and have found it an excellent introduction to retrieving feather. Once my puppy has proved that he will retrieve the covered pigeon I generally cut the stocking shorter so that the pigeon's head is free and so that he gets a look and a feel of the bird itself. Adhering to my principle of gradual progres-sive training, my next move would be to remove the stocking from the pigeon but I would tie the wings so that the puppy is more apt to learn to carry in a balanced manner rather than by dragging a bird by its wing. After this he can surely be tested on a cold bird in its natural state, but he does not want more than a few retrieves at a time or he will soon become bored and lose interest.

During the past few weeks whilst I have been giving my puppy his early retrieving lessons I will also have been giving him tuition on good behaviour on the lead. If one goes around any town or city in this country one is bound to see countless dogs that are virtually pulling the arms off their owners (I cannot fairly call them masters or mistresses!) How people can tolerate this sort of behaviour for at least ten years or more is beyond me. As far as a gundog is concerned, unless he is well nigh perfect on the lead I think one might just as well say 'goodbye' once he gets into the shooting field.

In another chapter, when describing the equipment I use for training, I said that I used a dog lead a little over 4 feet long (and this includes the loop). The importance of this should soon become apparent once one commences lead training. It should be understood that the puppy is always wearing a choke chain to which this lead is attached and that in these early stages I always hold the lead at its fullest length, because if one holds it short the tendency is for the puppy to pull even harder, and the trainer has nothing with which to play. I do not find it easy to describe exactly how I think one obtains the best results from this lead training because the method I use is more a matter of knack and of timing rather than physical effort. I always teach my dogs to walk on my left-hand side and for this reason I hold the lead at its fullest length in my right hand, chest high. As the puppy moves to pull I snap the lead with a downward chopping movement before he has time to pull it taut. The best description I can give of my elbow action is that it would be the same as if I were giving a neighbour a hard dig in the ribs. Each time I use this action I give the accompanying order 'Heel'. I need hardly add that dogs vary very considerably as to how long, or short, a time it may take before this method becomes effective.

My ultimate objective in this lead training is that I am enabled to walk my dog at heel fast or slow and that he should control his pace at all times in unison with mine. I also want him to do about turns smoothly and would expect the lead to hang slack always, whilst hanging on the index finger of my right hand which I hold chest high. After this he can be tested at walking heel-free. As in the case of all the other early lessons I would only teach him heeling in quiet surroundings where I can obtain his full concentration and I would not test him out amongst a crowd until he is much more mature.

## Chapter 6

# FORCE RETRIEVING

If I have any inhibition about writing this chapter it is
because I know that there are some trainers who are
more proficient at the job than myself. To be explicit,
they achieve their objective more rapidly. Yet I have
no hesitation in describing my own experience of force
retrieving, not only because the results have been 100
per cent successful but because I believe that the
trainer who lacks this knowledge can never feel fully
competent to deal with all the problems that may arise
in training spaniels. A spaniel that hunts but will not
retrieve is only half a gundog, and even those that are
'sometimes retrievers' are totally unsatisfactory. As I
have said I never use the force method unless every
other attempt has resulted in failure but, speaking
professionally again, if one is continually training dogs
for a living one would have too many non-retrievers, or
unreliable retrievers, unless one resorted to force
retrieving and no owner is satisfied with a gundog that
will not retrieve.

Throughout this book I have continually tried to
stress the fact that it is of little use to try and deal with

66

any aspect of gundog training in a half-hearted manner, and this is particularly so in the case of force retrieving. If one starts to use this method one is truly committed because if one gives up half way it is almost a certainty that the dog will never again even look at a dummy, or a bird. So, in the words of the late Sir Harry Lauder's famous song one must be prepared to 'Keep right on to the end of the road'.

For this lesson, in particular, I always try to choose a place of quietude where one can be assured of no distractions so that I can get the entire concentration of my dog. For reasons that will soon be apparent I wear soft shoes, or at least boots with rubber soles, throughout this exercise. Once we have arrived at a suitable place I make my dog sit on my left-hand side and, because I want him to remain sitting, I hold the lead short for this lesson only, in order to maintain this position. I also prefer him to wear an ordinary dog collar instead of the choke chain that I use for his other lessons.

The object of this exercise is to make the dog open his mouth and the most effective method is to place one's right instep on his off forefoot. The degree of pressure needed to achieve this varies very considerably with each dog but invariably it must produce a 'Yip'. Immediately he opens his mouth be ready with the tennis ball which should be held in the right hand, and place it in his mouth simultaneously to the order 'Take it'. I use a tennis ball in the early stages of force retrieving as it is easier to hold than a dummy. The antics that will result from this first introduction to force retrieving vary enormously between each individual dog. Some will attempt to turn somersaults (which should be restricted by the short lead), whilst others need considerable pressure to obtain the required mouth opening. To start with, of course, the dog will almost invariably drop the ball almost as soon as it is placed in his mouth, but one must persist and go through the same procedure already described until one is successful in getting him to hold the ball for at least a minute. During the time that he is actually holding the ball I speak to him occasionally, very quietly, telling him he is a 'Good dog' and I stroke him gently at the same time.

Assuming that I have been successful in getting him to hold it for a minute or so I then remove the ball to the order 'Gently', and then go through a similar procedure once again. But, since justice and common sense are the bases of all dog training, I present the ball to my dog a few inches in front of his muzzle each time that I give the order 'Take it', before I attempt any pressure with my foot.

I am well prepared for the fact that for many days, weeks, or even months, there will be no reaction from my pupil, but one must not be despondent, for the day will surely come. Certainly this exercise requires much patience and self-discipline on the part of the trainer but if one is consistent the end results should prove more than worth the effort. As near as is practically possible I like to continue this training every day of the week because if the task is adhered to consistently the objective will be achieved more promptly. I know that some trainers spend about 20 minutes on this operation daily. Personally speaking, I spend about 15 minutes a day, on average.

I could not possibly suggest just how long the job

will take because I have had dogs that reacted within ten days whilst others have taken as long as four months. But if one is consistent in following the training I have described, one day, when one presents the ball to the dog, he will make a grab for it immediately he is told to 'Take it', and this is understandably a thrilling moment. Here again the reactions will vary from dog to dog, because, whilst some will make a very positive grab for the ball, others will be more tentative. In either case I praise them profusely by telling them they are 'Good dogs', etc. One knows with certainty that the dog that grabs for the ball is going to be easy but with one that is tentative much care must still be taken and he will need every verbal encouragement each time that the ball is presented to him.

Once a puppy has proved that he will take the ball consistently on order, I teach him to do the same thing with a small dummy. My present aim is to get the dog to accept the dummy consistently to the order 'Take it' for about three days and then I think he is ready for the next stage.

It must be plain that one's objective is to get the dog to pick the dummy from the ground but here again I like to do this by a gradual process. If I have been successful in getting him to accept the dummy con-sistently for three days or so my next move is to find a box, some 8 inches high, on which I can place the dummy, but I first ensure that the box will remain steady by placing a brick, or any similar makeweight, beneath it. Normally the dog is reluctant to bend his head to take the dummy to start with, so I put some pressure on his head and neck with my hand in order to force him towards the dummy, ordering 'Take it' at

the same time. Once again there are going to be varia-
tions between each individual dog as to how rapidly, or
otherwise, this next step is accepted.

Once my dog has proved that he will pick up the
dummy consistently from the box to order I consider
that he is ready to take it from ground level. So the next
time I bring him out I hold the lead at its full length
and when I place the dummy on the ground I repeat
the order. To start with he will again be reluctant to
bend right down. I then place my right foot on the
slack of the lead in order to force his head down, and I
order 'Take it' simultaneously. Again the reactions are
bound to vary but the average dog will learn to pick the
dummy from the ground to order within a few days.

After this the task should be simplicity itself. I
simply place, or throw, the dummy a yard, or two yards,
in front of him and order 'Take it'. At this stage I
generally still have his lead on and I let him run free
with it. Once he is retrieving consistently I change the
order from 'Take it' to 'Fetch it', using the same tone.
My next step is to take him out in my lane where I
release him from the lead, and when I despatch him
to the order 'Fetch it' I encourage him to run in to each
retrieve. I give him from six to ten retrieves in order to
ensure that the message has gone home and I praise him
for each retrieve well done. I generally continue this
for six or seven days, after which I consider that he is
ready for the training on steadiness which I have already
described.

Those who have not yet attempted force retrieving
might well think that the dogs might show some resent-
ment but in my experience this has never been the
case. Indeed, after I have forced a dog no one has known

Page 71 Signalling for direction. The dog awaits command

Page 72 The signal given, the dog moves where directed

that he has had this training unless they have been told. And I do know that the dogs have been 100 per cent reliable as retrievers. In fact, I forced one delightful Labrador who became so keen that he was apt to grab my arm even before I was able to throw the dummy! He was a very reliable retriever in the end!

One never *asks* a forced retriever to retrieve but one should tell him quietly, but firmly, to 'Fetch it' and then he can be relied on to do the job consistently for the rest of his working days.

## Chapter 7

# PEN TRAINING

I count myself as very fortunate in that during the years since the war I have known two friends, both sporting farmers, who have generously allowed me to erect training pens on their land. Without this facility any professional trainer would be very hard pressed to do the job anywhere near efficiently. The value of a training pen to any serious trainer is inestimable. Within its confines one can teach a spaniel most of the basics of his job, hunting, steadiness and quartering his ground.

For the uninitiated, let me explain some details of the training pen itself. My present pen is about 120 yards long by 60 yards wide, and the wire netting, which is $1\frac{1}{4}$ inch mesh, is 6 feet high. The netting is buried, or sunk, a foot deep all round in order to counter burrowing by the rabbits, and the posts supporting the wire are about 8 feet apart. There is plenty of natural cover within the pen but there are also piles of sticks, strategically spaced, under which the rabbits can find cover, and there is also a warren in the centre of the pen to which the rabbits can bolt. Usually I like to have about a dozen rabbits within a pen of the size that I have described.

When I first take my dog to the pen I do so with an open mind, for although I will have already made an assessment of the puppy as an individual, I confess that I still cannot be certain of his reactions until I have seen him in there. Surprisingly enough I have seen spaniels that were so diffident about 'putting a paw wrong', so to speak, that I have had some difficulty in arousing their interest in the moving rabbit. In the case of the average puppy, however, the reactions are easily predictable. Whilst with the really bold puppies one can forecast their behaviour unerringly!

I cannot say just how other trainers first introduce a spaniel to the training pen because I do not know, but I can describe my own method. I attach a check cord (made from a strong rope clothes line) to the choke chain that the puppy is wearing. This cord is at least 15 feet long, allowing for an ample loop. When I first take the puppy inside I have the check cord fixed in my hand so that what is left is equivalent to the length of an average dog lead. I walk round the pen until the puppy sees his first rabbit and when the rabbit starts to run I let go of the check cord. Providing that I can see that the puppy is not going to catch the rabbit I purposely allow him to have a chase. This is naturally to arouse his basic hunting instincts and I only make a grab for the check cord if I see that he is too hot on the heels of the rabbit.

The first session is very brief, perhaps 5 minutes or even less, but with most puppies it will suffice to get them well and truly started as hunting dogs. The second time that I take him to the pen the procedure is just about the same but, after this, it is nearly always time to 'put the brake on'. Obviously I cannot be specific as to exactly when this should be applied as it will vary from dog to dog and so this must be left to the judgement and commonsense of each trainer. Once the puppy has seen a moving rabbit is when I really start to instil the order 'Hup'. If he ignores the order I grab the check cord promptly, thus bringing him to a halt with a jolt. Then I make him wait for at least half a minute before starting him off again to the order 'Seek on'.

In the case of the comparatively rare spaniel that is reluctant to hunt I simply remove the choke chain and allow him to run free. The only thing that one can do with a puppy like this is to take him round the pen until he does show interest in the moving rabbit, and encourage him all the way.

To return to what I can best call the average spaniel. After I have had him in the pen two or three times on the check cord I usually dispense with this and I let him run wearing just the choke chain and an ordinary lead. It is only with the very hard cases that I use the check cord for much longer, and I do not use it again with most spaniels throughout the rest of their careers. If the puppy does ignore my order to 'Hup' I catch hold of the lead as quickly as I can and I give him two or three sharp jolts on the choke chain, repeating the order simultaneously. Then I hunt him on and test him for steadiness once again. Very soon after this I dispense with the lead and choke chain and let him run free. I generally find that by this time most spaniels are 'getting the message' about steadiness.

It is about now that I first introduce my spaniel to the gun. The reason that I wait until this time before

I fire is because he will be far less likely to show any distress once he knows the counter attraction of hunting. Hence I wait until he is really keen on his hunting before I fire and for this reason I do not get many cases of gun-nervousness, or actual gun-shyness. Each time that I fire I give the order 'Hup', raising my hand simultaneously, and it has often surprised me how quickly most dogs seem to learn to drop to shot.

If the puppy shows that he is confident with the gun, and if he seems to be steady to shot when I fire, I throw out a dummy at the same time. I think it is vital that my puppy will retrieve a dummy consistently in the pen where there is the far greater counter attraction of the rabbits. If he should fail to do so he must be considered an unreliable retriever, and it follows that his pre-pen training has been inadequate. Each time that I fire and throw the dummy I make him wait for at least half a minute before sending him to the clear order 'Fetch it'. If the puppy ignores the dummy, or refuses to pick it up, the trainer should persist. Quite often a tweak of the ear, accompanied by the stern order 'Fetch it' will suffice, and if he does retrieve after this he should be well praised. But if he is still unwilling to co-operate I can only suggest that the trainer should resort to the semi-force, or force, retrieving methods already described, for I can never agree that a dog that refuses to retrieve a dummy in a rabbit pen can be called a fully trained, or reliable, gundog.

During all this early training on steadiness to fur, etc I will also have been teaching my spaniel the rudiments of quartering his ground. For the benefit of those who may not be familiar with the term I should like to explain the exact meaning of quartering. To be explicit, the spaniel that quarters his ground efficiently should hunt the ground methodically about 25 yards to the left and right of his handler, and within this distance. Ideally, he should do this with the minimum of guidance by whistle or verbal command. Very naturally no intelligent dog is going to work his ground as precisely as this if the conditions of the wind are not in his favour. Indeed if he did so he would just be an automaton and he would be missing game; but under ideal conditions he ought to work nearly as methodically as a windscreen wiper.

Here I have been describing the actions of a fully trained spaniel. How does one reach this stage of perfection? In the earliest days in the pen, as soon as I have established a certain steadiness, I make my first move to teach the puppy how to learn to quarter. When he has moved a rabbit, been steady to it, and watched it away I make my first attempt to 'pull' him away from the direction in which the rabbit has gone. When I say 'pull' in this case I do not mean physically, but I make every endeavour to turn him away from it, both by signal and comand. I call him by name and I give the order 'back', which is my command to come, and at the same time I try to wave him toward myself. If he moves off in the direction of the rabbit I order 'No' very firmly and, should he ignore me, the only thing to do is to go after him. At this very early stage he is still likely to be wearing the lead and choke chain and when I catch hold of the lead I remonstrate with him by giving two or three sharp jolts of the choke chain, repeating the order 'Back' at the very same time.

Once the puppy begins to acknowledge this order I make every endeavour to hunt him on in the opposite direction to which his last rabbit has gone and, in order to try and get this co-operation and understanding, I accentuate my actions as much as possible by pointing with my arm and hand in the direction that I want him to take. I make this signal as obvious as I can and I move in that direction myself. When he finds another rabbit I 'Hup' him and go through the same procedure once again, and although it will probably take a little time to achieve even this amount of co-operation one is at least forming the basis of quartering. By this time the puppy should be working free without the lead and his trainer should begin to make a genuine effort to get him to work to a pattern in his hunting, and when I use the word 'pattern' I mean this literally—right to left.

From now on, each time that I take the puppy to the pen I walk him quietly on the lead for about a minute outside the pen. I walk slowly and I include a couple of 'about turns' in order to get his concentration before we go inside. Once we are in the pen I make him sit and then I remove his lead and choke chain. Then, moving my arm in the direction in which I wish him to hunt, I give the order 'Seek on'. Because I want to accentuate the signal I not only step out in the same direction but I also make the fullest possible use of my hand, which I hold palm downwards, with fingers outstretched and held about hip high. When the puppy finds a rabbit, if he is steady to it, I do not keep him 'on the drop' for more than 10 to 15 seconds, then I give the order 'Back' and urge him to seek in the opposite direction by clear signals, etc. Should he ignore my command and my signal, however, I always come prepared with another deterrent to this sort of disobedience.

A puppy seems to learn very early in life that fleetness

of foot is his ally and hence that his speed over the ground is much faster than is a human's. At no time since the war have I ever been able to run after a dog owing to a leg injury, and I mention this because it has been more than ever necessary to outwit my spaniel in some way that will counteract this slight handicap. Of course, even if one were an Olympic runner, and a dog took off into the blue in a 20 acre field, one would be hard pressed to catch him!

To return to the point where I had my spaniel in the pen and where he had just ignored my command to turn. How best to make contact with him at range? I have not much doubt that the best way is to be adept with a catapult, when it would be easy to contact a dog at range. The missile should be a small potato or apple, or anything of similar substance that cannot cause physical damage but can result in a 'stinger' on a dog's retreating rump! Unfortunately I am not skilful with a catapult but, over the years, I have learnt a certain proficiency at making contact simply by throwing. Although I am bound to take this seriously, because I regard it as an important moment in a dog's career, I have never ceased to be amused at a puppy's expression at the moment that he first realises I am able to contact him at range. Up till then his attitude has doubtless been that of a child, 'Ha, can't catch me' sort of thing. But the moment that I do hit him his expression is one of complete bewilderment, awe and respect, as much as to say 'I had no idea you were as clever as that!' Undoubtedly this first contact at range has a very considerable psychological effect, and all the benefits are on the trainer's side. My 'ammunition' is small potatoes or apples, and if these are in short supply I carry a few small pebbles in my pocket. The moment that I throw is immediately after the order 'Back' has been ignored, and I repeat the order as I throw. Speaking from past experience I can only say that soon after the puppy learns that his master possesses this 'magic' he generally learns to comply with the order that is given. If 'master' is consistent about this the dog will begin to turn to order, and this is indeed a 'turning-point' in the puppy's career.

From now onwards some sort of true pattern should be taking shape. The puppy should be learning not only steadiness, and turning to command and direction, but he should also be ready to learn some of the refinements as well. If by now he is acknowledging the 'Back' and he is also following his trainer's hand signals, which means that he should be hunting in the direction indicated, he should be ready to learn to do this by whistle alone.

The whole basis of dog training is association of ideas, which is activated by the consistent sounds and actions of the trainer, and any ordinarily intelligent dog should soon learn to imbibe the commands and actions. If my puppy is already fairly consistent about acknowledging the order 'Back' I consider that he is now ready to turn to whistle. The whistle that I use for this purpose is the Acme Silent whistle and I hold this between my teeth like a pipe whilst I am handling him. Each time that I give the order 'Back' I follow the order with two short blasts on my silent whistle, as this is the sound that I wish him to associate with turning. It may take him a little time to take this in but after a week or two one can usually dispense with the verbal order and turn him to the whistle alone.

81

If the puppy has advanced satisfactorily in this progressive training let us now take a look at his present behaviour. He should have learnt to hunt for, and find, rabbits and be steady to them. He should be steady to shot, and he should retrieve the dummy consistently in the pen when he is bidden to do so. He should also be turning to the silent whistle, and therefore hunting his ground methodically, as opposed to 'pulling' forward. I like a puppy to learn to be 'handy' in the pen so that one can literally wave him into a bush by hand signal. I should also like to stress that if he does ignore my whistle, or the order 'Back', I do not keep on blowing my whistle, nor do I give an order more than twice, but I get after him and I give him two or three good tweaks of the ear and I repeat the order last given at the same time. Since this is a moment of truth he must be made to realise there and then that disobedience will not be tolerated. Indeed I would say that if the trainer vacillates here he is fighting a losing battle, and the puppy will realise this immediately.

In the same way that I taught the puppy to turn to two short blasts on the silent whistle I also want him to learn to stop to one long blast on the same make of whistle. If the puppy is of average intelligence there should not be much difficulty in teaching him to do this. Give one long blast on the whistle immediately after giving him the order 'Hup', raising one's arm and hand at the same time, as this is the signal to stop. After a bit of practice the puppy will learn to stop to the whistle alone.

In the previous chapter I tried to stress the vital importance of the tone in which commands are given, and that they should be both incisive and decisive.

The pen should be a place where the trainer should really be able to assert his authority because, if he is unable to establish his personality within this limited area, he has very little chance of maintaining it in the big spaces outside. Indeed if one requires a dog to perform well outside he needs to be nearly faultless in the pen.

During the past ten years or so several amateur trainers have brought their dogs to my pen for training. As an observer I could not help being critical of two things most of them did. Firstly, in several cases, they seemed so nervous about their dogs chasing a rabbit that they kept 'Hupping' them every few yards even before the dogs had seen or moved a rabbit. This has always seemed to me like dodging the issue. I have been apt to advise them to let their dogs hunt in a natural way and, if the puppies did have a chase, they could be given correction there and then. The second point that I could not quite agree with was that after their dogs had moved a rabbit, and been steady to it, the majority were apt to keep the dogs on the drop for a full two minutes or more. This unnaturally prolonged stop tends to spoil the rhythm in a spaniel's hunting. Most certainly if one were training a spaniel for field trials these prolonged stoppages would prove a great deterrent to the dog's style of hunting.

Earlier in this chapter I wrote that I had been fortunate in that I had had few spaniels that were gun-shy, or gun-nervous. I would not have it thought, however, that I am trying to overlook the few. In my view there is a very distinct difference between what I call a gun-shy dog, and one that is just gun-nervous. As I see it, the gun-shy dog is one that bolts for home as soon as he hears the gun, but the dog that is just nervous tends to back away when the gun is fired; and in the case of a spaniel it may well slow him up in his hunting, or else make him tentative about his retrieve.

With a truly gun-shy dog I can only suggest that one should resort to drastic methods in an attempt to overcome this fear. All I can suggest here is for the trainer to take his dog to the pen several times without the gun, and try to make him very keen on hunting; and, in this special case, actually chasing rabbits. Then once he is really keen, the gun can be introduced again and, if it does not trouble him, he can be re-trained on steadiness. The gun-nervous dog should not require such drastic methods to cure him although every care should be taken to gain his confidence. When I fire in the training pen, I generally use an Acvoke adaptor in my 12-bore gun. The blanks for this adaptor are made in two charges, heavy and light. Naturally, the light charge blanks are less noisy and these are the ones that I use when I am handling a puppy that tends to be gun-nervous. I do not fire right over him but wait until he is several yards away before firing, and then I give him one of two quick retrieves to keep him happy. If he does happen to run in to the retrieve before I despatch him I am more pleased than dismayed about this, since one can easily revert to training in steadiness once he is confident with the gun. The main thing with a puppy that is a bit gun-nervous is to try and keep him happy in his hunting and retrieving. Although he will probably need a refresher course on obedience and steadiness after he has overcome his timidity with the gun this should not prove much of a difficulty for the trainer.

## Chapter 8

# IN THE FIELD

It is one thing to 'contain' a spaniel within the restricted limits of a training pen and quite another to do the same thing in a 20 acre field outside. Dogs are not foolish and they are quick to realise that the unrestricted areas are ideal for 'trying it on' and quite a lot of them do! Nevertheless, I always regard this moment when I first test my dog in the big world outside the pen as one of the most interesting and challenging moments in training, because this is the time that one discovers how well, or otherwise, the pen training has been ingrained.

Unless the pen training has been thorough the rest is likely to go awry. Even if the rules of the pen have been well-instilled remember that the rules that applied in the pen should also be adhered to outside. 'Hup' *means* 'Hup', 'Back' or the double whistle means turn, etc—and not maybe! And if the puppy does disregard these orders he is simply being disobedient. For example, if the puppy has been steady to rabbits in the pen he should also be steady when the order 'Hup' is given, even in the case of the supreme temptation when he first sees a hare. Or else, if he turned consistently to the double whistle when hunting in the pen, he should also acknowledge this in the same way outside. If he continually disregards these well-known orders, what should be done?

Patently, these are moments that are 'win or lose' for the trainer and if he fails to do anything constructive about it there and then he may as well save himself the trouble of taking any other training seriously, as he will have lost his ascendance forever. For instance, I have always thought that the first run-in outside the pen is the one that really matters, and that if one does not nip disobedience in the bud at the time that it happens one might as well become reconciled to an unsteady dog for the future. This brings me to the thorny subject of correction and, when needed, how should it be applied?

I do not think that anyone is entitled to be so narcissistic about his own behaviour with dogs as to be certain that each move or action that he takes is not open to justifiable criticism. At the same time it seems fair to me that one can take into account the opinions of observers for whose judgement one has a certain respect, especially if these views are not biased. If this is acceptable I think that most fair-minded people would say that I am quite kind to gundogs in their training. If this is true, I am in no way complacent about it, for any trainer, be he amateur or professional, needs to be genuinely fond of dogs in order to train them, so that correction must be a distasteful task. Indeed, as far as the professional is concerned, he must be certain that he is justified in applying the correction, and at the right moment, or else his error can cost him very dearly by putting him weeks behind in training.

In the mid-thirties, when I started training, it was still not entirely unfashionable to hear the term 'Dog Breaking'. Thank goodness this expression is now obsolete and that everyone connected with gundogs nowadays regards this attitude as completely unenlightened. At the same time I can hold no brief for those who airily state that one should 'never hit a dog'. There can only be two sorts of people who could possibly make this vacant sort of statement: the fortunate few who have been lucky enough to have owned a couple of exceptionally tractable dogs that had been professionally trained, and those that were so addle-pated as to tolerate dogs that did exactly as they pleased. If, however, they said one should never hit a dog unjustly they would have my wholehearted support.

During the years that I have been training gundogs there have been many puppies that required some sort of physical correction only very occasionally, and this is exactly as I would have wished. Most of these have been of the sensitive type and therefore their 'punishments' have been appropriately mild. But, like any other professional trainer, I have also had to train dogs of extremely bold temperaments and, if one did not take a firm hand with them, such dogs would be completely out of control in no time.

When to correct a dog should be one of the simplest points in training, as it must be done as soon as possible after a known order has been disobeyed. This might fairly deal with the question of 'when', but it does not tell us 'how'. I do not want to take the easy way by simply using the cliché 'let the punishment fit the crime', since individual cases do not lend themselves to hard and fast rules.

87

Actually this old saying is most pertinent in that, before deciding just how the dog should be corrected, one must consider how errant was the crime. Some bold dogs blatantly ignore the order 'Hup' and go off into the blue after the hare, rabbit, or whatever, and others indulge in what I can only call a half-hearted run-in by going a comparatively short distance after the quarry. In the latter case I generally walk after them and, when I get hold of them, I slip the choke chain on and give them two or three sharp jolts, repeating the order 'Hup' at the same time.

With the really bold type of dog however, who takes to his heels and does a full blooded run-in, it is obvious that much sterner methods are needed if the trainer is to regain, and maintain, control. Ideally one should try to stop the dog in the act of running in but as he will be far too speedy this cannot be done. Instead, I simply walk steadily in the direction that he has taken and await his return. Almost invariably his expression will be contrite, and his steps toward me will be tentative, for he knows that he has done wrong.

I should have said enough already to prove that I would never countenance any sort of brutality towards dogs and I should like to reiterate that no trainer should ever correct a dog in a fit of temper. Yet, if a dog does commit a major error it is useless just to give him a couple of smacks for his waywardness. Any dog of this type will show no respect whatsoever for this inadequate punishment, and when he has the chance of repeating his misdemeanour he will do so immediately. It would be asking too much for me to attempt to be precise about the correction in this case, but a leather strap can do no physical damage and if this is applied to the culprit's

88

Page 89 Steadiness to fur—rabbits away, the dog halts

Page 90 The mark—a flushed rabbit is watched out of sight c
until shot

hindquarters in a moderate way it should suffice to show that bad behaviour will not be tolerated.

With regard to disobedience where quartering is concerned, a similar sort of correction should also apply. In the case of the puppy who only occasionally ignores the whistle, or the order 'Back', it will often suffice if one gets after him and admonishes him with a couple of tweaks of the ear, accompanied by two short blasts on the silent whistle. But the dog that persistently tries to take in too much ground will naturally need a heavier hand and in either case it is useless to blow, or to command, to no avail.

If I seem to have laboured over this matter of correction it is only because I regard it as vitally important. Any honest trainer must know that if he is to be the master in the true sense, correction is a part of training that cannot be ignored.

In an earlier chapter I said that I always liked to choose ground for training which favoured the job in hand and this is particularly true when I start a young spaniel hunting outside the pen. The type of ground that I have in mind here is a place where I am able to keep the puppy in view all the time that he is working, in fact every yard of the way. This may be sedge grass, sugar beet, or any ground where the cover is low enough so that I can see exactly what he is doing. I select these areas not because I want to keep him away from thick cover such as brambles, but because I want to be able to see that he is really learning to quarter his ground. As long as the puppy is in sight I can correct any error far more quickly than if he were out of view. There is also the advantage that the dog can see my hand signals. If I can find a place where the brambles are not very high, and not too profuse, I am very happy to work him in this sort of cover providing that he cannot get out of my sight for long.

Like any other professional trainer I do a great deal of my work during the summer and, for the sake of convenience, I shall pretend that the puppy I am training is ready for work outside the pen about midsummer. Clearly at this time of year one is very limited as far as shooting game is concerned, and this generally means taking the odd pigeon or rabbit. Whilst I would not want to seem to digress, nor to reminisce just for the sake of it, I should like to give a description of spaniel training before myxamatosis decimated the rabbit population. I have no doubt that spaniel training was a much easier job in the days when rabbits abounded and the reasons for this are not far to seek. When there were plenty of rabbits about, even if they had gone to ground, their scents were present most of the way which meant that there was something to keep a spaniel interested during most of his hunting. It was consequently much easier to keep him quartering his ground. But now that the pheasant is the main quarry the job is entirely different as one often has to go a considerable distance before picking up a scent. The bird may have run for about a quarter of a mile in a straight line and made it much more difficult to teach a spaniel to quarter.

Although I would be the last one to suggest that in field trials for spaniels it was an easy matter to get to the top twenty years ago, when the vast majority of trials were on rabbits, there is no doubt that it was a far less complicated business as far as retrieving was concerned. I should judge that in those days a 40 yard retrieve was regarded as quite good, but present-day spaniel trials are quite often like a minor retriever trial. Since one may well be asked to collect a blind retrieve, in an open stake, at a distance of 100 yards, one needs a dog that will really handle.

This digression should serve not only to describe the advantages of training spaniels where rabbits are plentiful but also to advise the trainer of some of the problems that he may well have to face owing to present day conditions. Personally, if ever I have the chance of working my spaniels on ground where there are rabbits I am very grateful for the opportunity, particularly so during the summer months. Unfortunately these opportunities do not present themselves very often nowadays and so one has to make the best of conditions as they are. The next best thing as far as I am concerned is to take my young spaniel into a field of sugar beet and work him down wind. Ideally I like it if there is the odd pheasant to put up and also, of course, the occasional rabbit or pigeon, which I can shoot for him. If my live cartridges have been unnecessary (which they are, more often than not!) I place the adaptor in my gun and fire a blank when my puppy least expects it and I throw a dummy out at the same moment.

In the sugar beet I am able to watch my young spaniel every yard of the way. Although I am glad if I can shoot a rabbit or pigeon, the actual shooting is secondary to giving the dog my entire concentration. Providing one does not relax he should be conscious of this all the way. My aim is to keep him going freely and happily but insisting at the same time that he quarters his ground properly. This does not mean that I nag him, for a dog that is constantly nagged soon becomes slow and confused. If my previous training has been thorough he should be well aware of my concentration and also of my determination not to tolerate disobedience. This awareness is the invisible cord that binds the dog to his trainer and if the cord is not strong it is almost invariably due to the trainer's lack of concentration. As long as he is working with me, acknowledging my hand signals to right and left, I keep my mouth shut and do not speak or blow my whistle, because this is how I want him to work. If the dog moves a bird, or a rabbit or hare, he shoud be steady but, if he is not, he needs the sort of correction already described. When he gets a retrieve I give two short blasts on a Staghorn whistle, simultaneous with the pick-up. This note or urgency tends to make him gather cleanly and also to hasten back with his retrieve.

I also give him intermittent practice at steadiness to the stop whistle, but only occasionally as I do not want to spoil the rhythm of his hunting. These training sessions usually last 10–20 minutes. Although this may not seem very long the factors that really count are the trainer's concentration and his ability to use every minute to get the best results. When training in summer the best times are early morning or in the evening, for one cannot fairly expect a dog to hunt hard, or retrieve well, in the heat of the sun.

When October comes I am eager to see how my trainees will perform at the real job. Despite this, before I take a young spaniel pheasant-shooting for the first time, I like to get hold of a dead pheasant and give him two or three retrieves in an open field. I do this because I have often found that if one asks a young dog to retrieve a freshly-shot bird that he has never encountered previously he will sometimes refuse to pick it up.

Whereas if he has a few retrieves at home, and gets the feel of the bird, he is far more likely to retrieve properly in the shooting field. Indeed I make it a rule to do this with any sort of bird such as duck, woodcock or snipe. As far as hares are concerned I like to get a leveret for a young dog to retrieve as a full grown hare is pretty awkward for a young spaniel, especially until he has had some practice.

Once again, the kind of ground where I like to work my spaniel is a place where I can watch him all the time, and also where he is able to mark a bird when it is shot. I do not like hedge hunting with a young dog as this naturally tends to induce him to hunt forward in a straight line, whereas I am still especially keen to encourage the quartering. I prefer to go out with an experienced gun who is interested in gundog work and to leave the shooting to him. There are two good reasons for this. First, it allows me to give my entire concentration to the dog, and secondly because I confess that I am a very indifferent shot! If I am lucky enough to get two retrieves I am well satisfied. When a bird is shot I make my dog wait for at least a full minute before sending him for the retrieve, because steadiness is all-important here. If game is scarce and scents are few I do not keep a young spaniel hunting for very long as he will become bored if there is no incentive. In either case I do not work a youngster for much more than half an hour. My aims are the same as in all the earlier training, efficient quartering, steadiness and clean retrieving.

Ultimately I like a spaniel automatically to be steady to shot, and also to fur and feather, when he moves them. If the dog is properly trained the handler should be capable of 'pulling' him away from the bird that has just flown, if it is not shot, by a mere wave of the hand in whatever direction he so chooses. Similarly, he should be able to draw him away from a marked retrieve if he does not want him to collect it. If he experiences any difficulty over this he cannot regard his dog as being under sufficient control.

Nowadays many of the big formal shoots do not begin pheasant shooting until November and when the time comes I am keen to give my dogs as much experience at picking up as I can. Very understandably the host is most interested in having dogs that are able to find and collect the difficult birds, so I like to take an older experienced dog, who is capable of getting runners, as well as a youngster.

When I first take a dog to a big shoot for picking up I always have him on a lead, not only to spare my blushes lest in all the excitement he should run-in in public but because he will not have had the experience of working in the company of another dog, since I only train them individually at home.

If one has the choice there are two places where one can stand, immediately behind one of the guns or 150 yards behind the line. Looking at it purely from the point of view of introducing a young dog to his first big shoots, which he can find pretty exciting, I prefer to be well behind the line to start with. When there are difficult birds to collect one can send the older dog for them but, with any luck, there should also be a few easy retrieves for the young one. If my trainee is reasonably well-behaved and shows no signs of gun-nervousness I like to take him right behind one of the guns and give him a few retrieves from there. One day there will be a chance of an easy runner, a bird that is hard-hit and does not run very far. Young dogs often jib when asked to retrieve their first live bird, especially if it is flapping. This is not a matter for much concern as it will be surmounted with time and experience.

## Chapter 9

# ADVANCED TRAINING

Whether in the shooting field or at field trials one requires a dog that will jump a fence to get his retrieve. Some trainers have jumping lanes which are naturally ideal for this purpose. These are generally about 6 feet wide and the enclosing wire netting is about 6 feet high. The jumps are graduated and get progressively higher, the first one probably being 1 foot high, the last about 3 feet 6 inches. I should judge that the spacing between each of the jumps is about 6 feet.

As I do not have a jumping lane I look first for a place where the obstacle is low, and when I throw my dummy over the other side I ensure that the dog has a good view of it. After a short wait I send him to fetch it and when he reaches the obstacle I give the command 'Over', which is the order that I want him to associate with jumping. After this it is obviously a matter of testing him over fences that are increasingly higher, but like everything else in dog training I believe that this should be a gradual process. There are far too many amateur trainers who try to run before they can walk properly as far as training is concerned which only causes confusion and despair in the minds of the trainees. The main thing when teaching a young dog to jump is for him to succeed, because the more often he is successful the better he will become at the job. Once he is proficient at retrieving over some of the higher jumps, about 3 feet 6 inches, the trainer should gradually increase the distance from which the dog is sent. To start with, for instance, he can be sent from about 5 yards behind the fence, but once he is confident the distance can be increased by stages. It is very important to take every opportunity to impress the command 'Over' by repeating it each time that the dog approaches the fence. If he does hesitate and look back to his trainer he needs every possible encouragement. The trainer should show the whole palm of his hand to him, and use a pushing action, as if he were literally propelling the dog over the fence. This action must always be accompanied by the command 'Over'.

The dog will thrive on encouragement and he deserves every praise for a retrieve well done. Once he is confident about jumping and really understands 'Over', he can be tested on a blind retrieve over the fence, encouraged by the order 'Hi lost', a command which I describe more fully below.

*  *  *

Strictly speaking, I suppose that teaching a dog to hunt for several retrieves in cover does not come under the heading of advanced training. But since I want to try to write in sequence, and because it is the basis of some of the advanced training, I am including the matter in this chapter.

First I take the dog to a place where the cover is low, such as tufted grass or low bracken or heather, because

I want him to have a clear view when I throw more than one dummy. At the beginning I just use two dummies but once he has learnt to collect these satisfactorily I add a third. This is the time that I really start using the order 'Hi-lost'. Candidly, I wonder if this should rightly be called an order, for more often than not it is used as a term of encouragement when the dog is hunting for a lost bird. I suppose that it is really a matter of the tone in which it is given but, like most handlers, I try to accentuate the sound by urging my dog to 'Hi-lost' when he is hunting. This is one of the few occasions that I can think of when the handler is entitled to be loud. Others may be when he is encouraging the dog to jump 'Over', and when using the command 'Get out' for a distant retrieve.

Once the dog has shown that he is efficient at collecting several retrieves, after he has seen them thrown into cover, I am ready to test him out on some blind retrieves. I leave the dog in his kennel whilst I put the dummies out and, at first, I do not make them too difficult to find because, above all else, I want him to succeed. When I bring him out I tell him to 'Hi-lost' and if he finds and retrieves all three dummies successfully I praise him well. After this I place the dummies out so that they are progressively a bit more difficult to find, varying the sort of cover in which they are placed, and I continue this kind of training until the youngster is really keen on his hunting for unseen retrieves.

\*           \*           \*

The next training lesson can legitimately be included in a chapter on advanced training in that my objective is to teach my dog to hunt for an unseen retrieve when he has already marked an obvious retrieve in a different direction. This is clearly a test of control, for one's aim must be to direct the dog so that he hunts for, and finds, a blind retrieve before he is allowed to collect the one that he has already marked.

It may well be that there are several different methods for teaching a dog to do this but personally I am all for trying the comparatively easy way to start with. In an earlier chapter I described how I make the best use of the lane down which I live, with its high hedges, and here again it has its advantages. Like most hedges it has certain gaps, with one particular place giving ample access to a small area of ground that is covered with sedge grass and low brambles, and it is in here that I place my blind retrieve. When I bring my dog out I throw a dummy straight down the lane in full view of him. There are only two directions in which he can possibly go: straight ahead to collect the dummy that he has marked, or to the gap in the hedge to my right hand side. For this first lesson I stand about a yard behind him and, making the best possible use of hand and arm, I indicate that I want him to hunt to my right, to the orders 'Seek in' and 'Hi-lost'. Very naturally the dog's inclination will be to go for the marked retrieve and if he moves off in that direction I give the two orders 'No' and 'Hup' sharply. Then I order him to 'Back' and I insist on his hunting the cover to my right for the blind retrieve. Should he happen to defeat me the first time by collecting the marked retrieve first, I am even more vigilant the second time and am prepared to 'catch him one' with my apple, potato or pebble, if he moves off in the wrong direction.

Once the dog has proved that he is learning this new

lesson I can afford to stand a bit further behind him when sending him for his blind retrieve. Then he can be tested in an open field where I usually use a couple of tennis balls. When we get into the field I cover the dog's eyes with my hand so that he cannot see and I throw one ball to my right, or to my left. Removing my hand, I throw the other ball straight out, let him mark it, and then insist on his hunting for, and collecting, the unseen retrieve first.

The next aspect of training, which I regard as an essential, is one that I have heard a few trainers argue against. In writing this book I have stressed the importance of control in every forseeable circumstance, and I believe I can give two practical examples of when and where the training I am going to describe is a vital necessity. This particular training is a test of control as it involves being able to stop a dog in his tracks after he has been despatched for a retrieve, and then ordering him back before he collects it. To a mild degree I can follow the reasoning of those trainers who suggest that this sort of training 'pulls a dog off his mark' with the result that the dog will become a poor marker. Certainly if the handler were so lacking in common sense as to make a practice of doing this every time that he sent his dog for a retrieve the net result would be that he would be a very indifferent marker. No thoughtful handler would do this, but there are times when he could be very glad of this extra control. At a big shoot, for instance, one may have despatched the dog for a retrieve and suddenly another wild, uncontrollable dog appears from out of the blue with a clear intent of grabbing the same retrieve. Naturally, if the handler has the ability to stop his dog in its tracks and call him back this

unfortunate collision, with its sometimes dire consequences, can be avoided.

Again, if I may reminisce for a moment, there was one
special occasion at field trials several years ago when I
was very glad that I had this control over my dog. The
dog that was working under the other judge put up a
pheasant, which was shot, and the handler was told to
send his dog for it. For some obscure reason my judge
told me to send my spaniel for the same retrieve at
almost the same moment. He then realised his mistake
and calmly told me to 'bring her back'. When I received
this last order my bitch was already 30 yards away, going
flat out in the direction of the retrieve, but I was still
able to pull her up on my stop whistle and bring her
back to heel. Candidly, I do not think that I have had
many dogs that would have proved so biddable,
especially amid the stresses of a field trial.

When I am training a dog to do this I take him out in
an open field. After making him 'Hup' I walk out ahead
of him and ensure that he marks the dummy when I
place it at least 35 yards away. Then I walk back to him
and place myself right beside him. As he moves off to the
order 'Fetch it' I step forward simultaneously and order
'Hup', and if he stops I back away from him and order
'Back'. The second time I order 'Fetch it' I will go
through the same procedure but, providing that all has
gone well, I will let him go all the way for the retrieve
the next time.

If the dog is what I can best describe as an 'especially
hot one' I have even reverted to putting him on the lead
and choke chain when I despatch him so that I can grab
the lead should he ignore the order 'Hup'. Thankfully
there are not many dogs who make me resort to this. As

for the others, I decrease the distance of the retrieve whilst I increase this distance that I let them go before stopping them but, as in all the other training, this is a very gradual process.

\*             \*             \*

I confess that I have some inhibitions about writing on 'training a dog to mark' for although it may sound like over-simplification, I think that some dogs are natural markers, as if to the manner born. Although a trainer can take certain steps to foster, and to improve, a dog's ability to mark I find that basically it is a matter of the dog's eyesight and range of vision. Obviously there is nothing to compare with experience, and if one is able to take a dog picking up in open country where he has every possible opportunity to mark the flight and fall of birds this is bound to increase his ability. It is helpful to a young dog, particularly in the early stages of his training, if one uses a white dummy in order to increase his ability to mark. I also think that a trainer can make very good use here of the dummy launcher, which I described earlier. The dummy supplied with the launcher is off-white, and if this is fired in open country it provides good training in teaching a dog to mark as it has the advantage that it can be aimed so that the dummy will drop at distances that can be increased gradually.

\*             \*             \*

Rightly or wrongly I regard the next exercise as the ultimate as far as advanced training for a spaniel is concerned. For want of a better term I am apt to call it the 'three ball trick' although I know only too well that this is a misnomer. It is certainly no trick, but a very valuable and, as far as I am concerned, logical part of training.

First I take the dog out in an open field where I order him to 'Hup', and I then walk diagonally across the field to his right. When I have walked about 100 yards away from him I call his attention by making high-pitched noises. Once he is really looking my way I toss the ball up several times so that he sees it and then drop it on the ground. I walk back to him, taking up position about 10 paces to his rear. When I have his full attention I raise my right arm to the perpendicular position, the palm of my hand foremost with fingers extended, and only then am I ready to despatch him. As I give the order 'Fetch it' I take a step to my right and bend from my hips in unison, whilst keeping my arm extended. This physical indication is the one that I want my dog to recognise when I am handling him on to distant retrieves. If the dog is successful in finding and retrieving the ball I only give him the one retrieve per day but I continue this training constantly in a direction to his right for a fortnight. Once I am confident that he has the message about getting out for his retrieve to the order 'Fetch it' I change the order to 'Get out', because this is the command that I want him to learn in relation to distant retrieves.

The next step is to teach him to do exactly the same to his left and in order to do this I go through the same sort of procedure in this direction. Although there are some handlers who handle their dogs very successfully ambidexterously, when I am teaching a dog this particular lesson, I still use my right hand and arm to direct him to the left. This involves taking a step to the left diagonally and swinging from the hips in the same direction whilst the right hand and arm is extended skywards. Once again I try to continue this training daily for another fortnight. I should add that I prefer to use new white tennis balls for this lesson since they are easier for the dog to mark when I call his attention from a distance of 100 yards.

After this I teach him to retrieve the ball at the same distance straight ahead. After making him sit I walk 100 yards straight ahead of him and each time I do so I throw the ball up until I am sure that I have his attention before dropping it. Then I walk back to about 10 paces behind him. Again I raise my hand and arm to the perpendicular and, using what I can best describe as a pushing action, I tell him to 'Get out'. Similarly, I continue this straight ahead training for about a fortnight.

Now comes the acid test, the whole object of the exercise, when the trainer will discover whether or not the previous repetitive training has been fruitful. I leave the dog in his kennel, or else in my car, whilst I place a tennis ball in the middle of the field, and 100 yards from where I intend to despatch him. To ensure that I get just the right place and distance I place a marker exactly where I mean to send him from. When I bring him out I 'Hup' him beside the marker and I bring two tennis balls with me. Then I take not more than 4–5 paces to his rear and I throw one ball as far as I can to his right and the other to the left. My objective is to try and 'push' him straight out for the 'blind' retrieve before allowing him to collect the two that he has marked. Now, of course, I make every possible endeavour to capture his concentration on my hand as

Page 107 Clear directions when hunting and a confident response

Page 108 (*above*) Champion in the making? Eager to go but awaiting orders; (*below*) The look of a champion—kind, keen calm and knowing. FT. CH. Lytchmore Hamers Jean, second in the Spaniel Championship, handled by the author

raise it to give my signal. As I give the clear order
'Get out' I try as hard as I can to give him one similarly
obvious 'push' with my hand and arm. Despite this,
almost invariably most dogs will start to move off in the
direction of the last retrieve they have marked. I am
prepared for this and as soon as my trainee does so I
give him the orders 'No' and 'Hup' as soon as he has
gone a few paces. I then order him 'Back' to his original
position and try again.

In attempting to describe my actions in training a
dog to this exercise it would be nonsensical to try and
be too specific because here, in particular, one needs to
be perceptive enough to adapt the training in accor-
dance with the behaviour of each individual pupil. If
I find that my dog tends to persist in going for one of
the marked retrieves I have, perforce, to take several
steps forward until these two marked retrieves are
behind me. After this I must persist until I am successful in making him 'Get out' to collect the blind retrieve
first. When he does so I naturally give him adequate
praise. Assuming that this is the general pattern for the
next few days of training I consider that I should be
able to 'read' my dog well enough to know whether I
can now take a few paces backwards when I despatch
him for his blind retrieve. Providing that he has been
well-praised for collecting the blind retrieve, before he
has been allowed to retrieve the marked ones, an
intelligent dog will soon learn the sequence after a few
days practice. Hence, this will allow the trainer to take
few paces further backwards until he reaches
the stage when he can place himself 10 or more paces
behind the dog when he throws the two tennis balls to
the right and to the left. By now he should be able to

push his dog straight out for the blind retrieve with every confidence.

Speaking from past experience the day that one is able to do this is indeed a red letter day for the trainer

The subject now is the use of the whistle, and to parody the immortal bard 'To blow or not to blow, that is the question'? As far as I am concerned there should be no question, for surely one should only blow when there is some purpose in blowing! As I write this seated in the comfort of an armchair, at least I have the grace to blush when I consider how often I have been as guilty as the next man of blowing my whistle not only uselessly, but also at the wrong moment. think that most of us, if we are honest with ourselves know only too well when we have handled a dog badly and have failed to do him justice. I referred earlier to a high-ranking soldier who accepted my advice over the faulty retrieving of his spaniel. The reason I mention this gentleman again is that he is the only person I have ever met who wrote a résumé on field trials, not from the view point of criticising the performance of other people's dogs, but of his own dog, and his own handling, in particular. Unfortunately not so many of us are quite so honest with ourselves.

I will readily admit that I have done a great deal of pre-training in my armchair. To be more explicit, when I have had certain problems with a trainee I have tried to work out my 'campaign' before I take him out for training. Sometimes this has proved successful, some times not, but I think that this can legitimately be called 'advance training'! I have also held many 'post mortems' in my armchair in an endeavour to work out just where things went wrong.

But to return to the subject of the whistle and its uses. As I write I am all too conscious of how much easier it is to say what should, and should not, be done and how much more difficult it is to put these precepts into practice when the time comes. In the heat of the moment we are all liable to do thoughtless things when handling and these errors are very confusing for the poor dog. I have read a great deal in the sporting press about over-use of the whistle and I have witnessed this more often than I care to remember. Indeed I have seen and heard some handlers giving a fair imitation of 'Macnamara's band'. Naturally their dogs paid no attention whatsoever as this cacophany had long since ceased to have any meaning for them.

However, if the dog has been trained in a thorough and thoughtful way, it should not be so difficult to decide when to use the whistle. If the dog has been trained to fetch a blind retrieve before he collects a marked retrieve, and if he has been trained on the three tennis balls as I have described, he should be well aware of his master's signals, to right or left, or straight ahead. And if he has been properly trained he should be absolutely steady to the stop whistle. If a blind retrieve is straight ahead and the dog moves off to the left or right one would naturally use the stop whistle but if he is hunting in the general direction of the retrieve it is usually best to leave him alone. When one is handling a dog on to a distant retrieve it is mutual understanding between the handler and his dog that really counts. I recall that when I was handling the best spaniel I have ever trained on to a distant retrieve her behaviour was telepathic. I could not count the number of times when she was fairly close to the retrieve and I was on the point of raising my whistle to my lips to give her a final signal and then she would turn in the right direction before I had time to blow

A final word about hand signals. There are quite a few people at spaniel trials today who seem to handle their dogs in the general direction of a retrieve with what I can only describe as a flapping sort of action, as if they were waving goodbye. I will admit that some of them seem to achieve the desired result but it never looks very convincing to me. Alternatively there are a few others, very few, who handle their dogs with an arm that is erect, with the full palm in view and fingers outstretched. These control their dogs with their hands. This is certainly the sort of handling I admire most.

I have known of trainers who supposedly taught their dogs water work by literally throwing them in the deep end. These people simply threw the dogs into water where they were obliged to swim. This has never been my approach to the job because, like the rest of the training, I prefer to do it gradually and to obtain the trainee's confidence.

About a mile from my cottage is a stream which I have found ideal for introducing a dog to water. The place where I go first is really a ford and the distance across is about 12 feet. Even at the centre of the stream the water is not more than a foot deep, so that there is no need for the dog to swim. First I throw a dummy that will float not more than 2 feet from the bank, and most puppies are willing to fetch it from this short distance. I then throw it a little further each time and, in many cases, I have succeeded in getting them to retrieve from the other side the first time that I take them there.

112

I always take an older dog with me that is used to water because if I get one that is reluctant to enter I have found that is of great help if he sees another dog that goes in boldly. I always wear gum boots for this job and if I have a youngster that is obviously a bit scared I wade in to the stream and try to entice him to follow me on the lead, but if he still drags back I do not try to force him. This sort of puppy will understandably need time, and patience, to get him over his fear but once he has gained enough confidence to fetch a few very simple retrieves near to the bank he should overcome this gradually.

As for the puppy that enters the water boldly in places where he is not required to swim I try and find a place where the ground slopes gradually and I throw the dummy out so that it is just out of his depth. If he gets it and does not show any fear of swimming, I throw it out a little further each time. Should he prove reluctant to swim, however, I have to try something else. I find a place where the water is near to the top of the bank and lift the dog into the water. Then I catch hold of the scruff of his neck and walk along the bank, bent double, until he learns that he is capable of swimming. In this sense it is rather similar to teaching a child to swim with a harness in a swimming bath. After the puppy has swum a few yards, and climbed up on the bank, I lift him back into the water and I throw a dummy not more than a yard ahead of him. If he retrieves this successfully I make much of him. If one increases the distances of the retrieves very slightly each time his confidence should grow each time that he succeeds.

Many young dogs that are willing to swim out into

a stream for a retrieve show reluctance when they are asked to retrieve from the opposite bank. In order to teach them to do so I put on a pair of waders and I choose a part of the stream that is deep enough for my dog to have a swim, but shallow enough for me to stand in my waders at its centre. I also choose a place where the farther bank is not a steep one. Then I wade out into the centre of the stream with my dog at my side and throw a dummy on the edge of the opposite bank and I tell him to 'Fetch it'. If he does retrieve to me as I remain midstream I praise him and then I throw it a little further. After this I simply retreat a bit further each time until he has finally learnt to retrieve from bank to bank.

*Chapter 10*

# FIELD TRIALS

Many shooting men have never attended field trials and some people seem to be under the delusion that trials are artificial affairs. So for those who do not know what goes on I should like to describe a spaniel trial.

The average trial lasts two days, one day for the novice stakes and one for the open. Under present rules only thirty-two dogs are allowed to compete, so enabling the judges to give each dog a fair test, and this generally means that there are sixteen dogs running in each stake. I should add that present dog trials are so popular that it is no unusual thing for there to be more than forty entries for a sixteen dog stake, and therefore one needs to be lucky in the draw.

At spaniel trials there are only two judges and a referee who is called in at the end if the judges are unable to agree. On average there are six guns, all guests of the donor of the ground, and these gentlemen do all the shooting.

The ground and the cover will be the same as one would encounter on an ordinary shooting day, bracken, brambles, sedge grass, roots, etc. Two spaniels work at the same time, one under each judge. The dogs' job is to quarter their ground within range, to find game and to prove their steadiness. The dog must be rock steady when he moves or sees game, fur or feather, and if he moves as much as a few yards the judge will count this as a run-in and the dog is out. When a bird, rabbit, or hare is shot the dog must remain steady until the judge tells the handler to send him for it. When the dog is sent he must collect it as quickly and cleanly as possible and he must deliver it tenderly to hand.

The judges will be looking for the dog that has plenty of drive, that works his ground methodically, faces cover boldly and finds game. They should also be looking for the dog that does these things with the minimum of assistance from the handler, by command or whistle. When a bird is shot they will take note of how well the dog marks the fall, wherever this is possible, and when he retrieves they will be watching to see if he retrieves it cleanly, without mouthing it or dropping it. They will also be watching the delivery of the retrieve, as to whether it is brought right up to hand, or dropped sloppily at the feet of the handler. They will also examine each bird, rabbit or hare closely, to see if they have been damaged in transit.

Where a dog is sent for a blind retrieve the judges will observe how well, or otherwise, he handles out to the fall. If a dog is sent for a comparatively simple retrieve a judge can only allow a few minutes for its collection or else he would never have time to do justice to the rest of the competitors. In the case of a runner, particularly a strong one, any competent judge will give a dog every reasonable chance to succeed, especially when he has shown that he has taken the line.

When a spaniel is hunting at a trial if he 'pegs' a bird, rabbit or hare he can be eliminated. Pegging is when a dog catches a bird, for example, that has not been shot and if he retrieves it to his handler he will be eliminated. Should he peg a bird, however, and he releases it immediately on command from the handler, some judges will give him a second chance. My own view is that this is the right thing to do, particularly so if it is early in the season when the cover is thick and there are young birds about.

Every dog has a run under each judge, unless they have been eliminated on their first runs for any of the reasons I have already described. After the judges have seen all of the dogs they require there is usually a 'run off' between some of the dogs that have so far put up the best performances. These run offs vary in number according to the judges on the day but, on an average, I should say that from two to six dogs are usually called in for this further judgement. If one is competing it is sheer folly to become too elated even if you have done well in the run off because the judges may already have another dog 'on ice'. The latter is a dog that has already had two exceptionally good runs under both judges and they have already decided that he is the winner, unbeknown to the handlers in the run off who are just competing for second, third and fourth places. Hence it is foolish to try and make any decisions about the results until they are read out at the end of the stake.

Should the judges find that two or three dogs are about equal in the run off they look for the dog with the most style. I find style very difficult to describe. Put crudely, a stylish dog should have a fluid action that is attractive to watch. To be slightly more analytical when,

in a fluid movement, the dog's rump moves left whil
his stern moves right (and vice versa) this is ver
pleasing.

One other point that I should like to mention i
relation to judging is on the subject of hard mouth.
have no intention of trying to influence judges, who ar
doubtless far more knowledgeable on the subject tha
myself, as to how to arrive at the right decisions. Speak
ing as a competitor I have found that the vast majorit
of judges are scrupulously fair in this matter and, i
there is any doubt, they invariably give the dog a secon
chance. For all this I have never been able to erase th
memory of something that happened at a trial over te
years ago. No one could accuse me of bias because i
this instance my own dog was not involved and I wa
just a spectator. One of the judges was obviously ver
'hot' on hard mouths because he had already put thre
dogs out for this reason. Then a bird was shot at prett
short range and landed with a loud clump on a larg
expanse of bare rock. When the dog retrieved it he wa
eliminated for hard mouth. Surely this was a ver
doubtful judgement?

Spectators at a field trial are always requested t
follow a steward who carries a flag. Unfortunately th
view varies very considerably according to the sort o
country in which the dogs are working. In some place
such as low bracken, or sugar beet, spectators should ge
an excellent view of the proceedings, but in others, lik
rhododendrons, or high brambles, it is very hard to tel
what is happening.

It is almost an impossibility to try and describe th
atmosphere at field trials to anyone who has not actuall
competed. I am sure that competitors in any kind o

sport get the 'butterflies' when they are waiting to participate. One is particularly conscious of this sinking feeling at field trials especially if one has drawn one of the higher numbers and must wait for a couple of hours before being called in. A man who had ridden in the Grand National was supposed to have remarked that handling a dog at a trial was even more exciting, although I think that this must be a bit of an exaggeration!

Often the handler has only about a 10 minute run in which to show the judge the dog's capabilities and since a good trial dog requires to have plenty of drive these can be very exciting moments. One may be sent for a retrieve in a hot corner where there are plenty of unshot birds and both handler and dog are required to 'keep their cool'. If one runs at field trials regularly there are bound to be times when one will get depressed after a bad run and nothing seems to go right. This can happen to anyone and certainly everyone needs a bit of luck to win trials. But it is also true that if one has a good dog, and luck, one is bound to get there in the end.

Unfortunately field trial conditions cannot be reproduced at home and even though a day's shooting can be quite exciting it is still not the same as a trial. A dog is very conscious of the competitive atmosphere, even during the long frustrating intervals when he is awaiting his turn, and he is well aware that his handler is keyed up too. The only advice I can give to the novice handler is that once he gets in the line, he should 'lose' himself with his dog so that he is not conscious of anything, or anyone, else. If he handles the dog properly this is all he will have time to do, but if he loses concentration he is sure to lose contact with his dog.

During the years that I have been competing at trials there have been several amusing incidents to relieve the tension. One such light-hearted moment occurred a few years after the last war. In a special stake confined to Clumber Spaniels, one of the dogs, handled by a very well-known professional, was sent to collect a cock pheasant. It was not a long retrieve but the bird had fallen behind a bramble bush and the judge did not have a clear view of it. The handler had a far better view and when, after a few minutes, the judge asked 'Has he got it, Jimmy?' the reply was 'He's not only got it, but he's nearly had it.' The dog had eaten the bird! (Lest I should offend any Clumber owners by telling this tale, I would never suggest that this behaviour is characteristic of the breed!)

But it is the competitors themselves who really make spaniel trials so enjoyable and any novice running in his first stake, can be assured of a fair reception. The judges will treat him fairly, and with understanding. If he wisely seeks advice from the leading professionals, or from the most successful amateurs, he will generally receive this unstintingly.

Until comparatively recently, say twenty years ago, I think I would be right in saying that it was a rare thing to see a lady handling a spaniel at a trial, but this is no longer the case. The general attitude used to be that the average spaniel would be too much of a handful for a lady to train and handle but this has been disproved on many an occasion since. Whether it is because lady handlers have been influenced by the successful invasion by women in so many other fields, or else because present day spaniels are more amenable to training, I would not care to try and judge. But the one inescapable fact is that the ladies have won a great many open stakes in recent years. Indeed the spaniel championship of 1973 was won by a dog that had been both trained and handled by a lady, the first time a lady had won it. The dog was Dr Diana Bovill's FT. CH. Hawes Silver, a great credit to her owner-handler.

I can look back to the years before the last war when spaniels were still regarded by so many as 'wild, uncontrollable dogs'. Although I am sure that we breed many more amenable spaniels nowadays I refuse to believe that the dogs that were bred forty years ago or more were all so intractable. What I do think is that there were comparatively few people at the time who had the necessary knowledge to train them properly. Most certainly the present day field-trial-bred English Springer is a very tractable animal. As evidence of this I have just recorded some of the successes that the ladies have had with this breed and if further proof is needed some octogenarians still have their triumphs too. I can think of three professionals, all in their eighties, who still handle their spaniels very successfully at trials.

It had been my intention to mention not only some of the most successful competitors in field trials, but also some of the outstanding personalities of the past and present, but I was soon forced to realise that I was faced with an *embaras de richesse*. I had to admit that if I started to mention a few I should be unjust to others and so I reluctantly decided to name hardly anyone at all.

For all this there must be an exception to every rule, and when one considers the fact that John Kent, still going strong in 1973, won his first stake in 1905 it is sufficient to make most of us look like a group of novices! His name was synonymous with spaniel trials

121

before most of us could remember. Quiet, modest, and efficient to a degree, he was generous to a fault throughout his career in his appreciation of the performance of a fellow competitor's dog. Over the years there must have been many occasions when he wondered at the judges' placings but only once did I hear him quietly remark that he did not agree. I haven't the least doubt that there were valid reasons for this statement!

Although I am determined to keep names to a minimum no account of spaniel trials, as I have known them, would be anything like complete without a reference to Joe Greatorex. All of us who attended trials over twenty years ago remember Joe's famous O'Vara Springers, then in the ownership of the late Mr Selwyn Jones. Certainly if one was competing against them there was good cause to remember, for they were very hard to beat. I am glad to say that Mr and Mrs Greatorex were still taking an active interest in field trials, as spectators when these words were written. I should add that countless pedigrees of the present day winners at trials go back to the O'Vara strain, which may well account for the tractability of some of the most successful dogs of today.

These two great professionals, together with the late John Forbes and Reg Hill, were the trainers who won so many of the major awards when I first ran at trials in the late thirties.

I shall not involve myself in naming today's most successful competitors for if I started to mention the leading professionals and the most accomplished amateurs, it would begin to read like a *Who's Who* in gundogdom. Anyone interested can soon find this out by referring to the sporting press.

No account of field trials would be anything like complete without attempting to do justice to the indefatigable secretaries of the different spaniel societies. These ladies and gentlemen voluntarily take on a task that I would never have the courage to do. They are all diplomats in the truest sense and if I were to describe the many kindnesses they have shown to me personally it would be a lengthy task. Apart from dealing with a large amount of correspondence they find suitable venues for the trials, which in itself is far from easy today. They also welcome the newest members and do everything possible to give them encouragement.

Field trials have their critics and no one would pretend that everything is perfect. Some people suggest that because the dogs often run for only 10–15 minutes this is no test of stamina and that they would be unable to last out a long day's shooting. It should be obvious that it is a mathematical impossibility for the judges to give most of the dogs longer runs as they would not have the time to see all of the dogs, particularly on a short winter's day. Yet this does not mean that the dogs that are competing are incapable of surviving a day's shooting, and most of them do so. I have talked to several of the leading professionals who all agree that the dogs they prefer to shoot over are those that they have made field trial champions.

During the past five or six years there have been a great many newcomers to spaniel trials and this is a healthy sign. A good many of these people have 'graduated' from competing in summer gundog tests to field trials. Whilst I think that gundog tests have done some good as 'nursery schools' for novices I have my reservations about them. Sometimes they seem to be too artificial and some of the tests are not always related to normal every day shooting. Although it is good to see new faces at trials I feel that in some cases it has lowered the standard of handling and I do not think that the standard is as high as it was ten years ago. Doubtless, once the newcomers get a bit more experience, this will adjust itself.

But even if field trials served no other purpose they suffice to show the general public the high standard to which gundogs can be trained. As well as this the people who breed field trial dogs select strains that will produce tractable, intelligent, courageous gamefinders, that have tender mouths, and this inevitably means that there are a great many more efficient gundogs being bred.

The ambition of all competitors at trials is to qualify for the spaniel championship at the end of the season and in order to do so one must be placed first or second in an open stake, which is no easy achievement in itself. The next objective is to win a diploma, to be placed, or to win the championship, which is even more difficult! The competitors come from every part of the country. There is always a strong Scottish contingent and, in recent years, there has often been a strong challenge from the Irish. Indeed in 1963 an Irish dog won the championship for the first time, and he was a very worthy winner. This was Mr J. McKelvey's FT. CH. Ruff in Tuff and I have good reason to remember this as my own Springer was lucky enough to be placed second.

I know that there are many people who do not agree with me but I still think that the championship can sometimes be a bit of an anti-climax if one studies it from the viewpoint of the performances of some of the competitors. There have been several instances when I consider that the dogs were putting up a much higher standard of performance early in November than they were when they ran at the championship. If this is the case, is it because some of these dogs have run at too many trials throughout the season, so that they are past their peak for the championship? I know that on the few occasions that I have been away from home for a whole week, running at three successive trials, my dog has always needed some re-training at the end of this time!

In an earlier chapter I wrote nostalgically of the days when spaniel trials were run mostly on rabbits and although I still enjoy trials immensely there are some things about the 'old days' that I miss. I regret the passing of the brace, and team, stakes that were a feature of trials at the time. Frank Middleton handled a very good team of English Springers owned by the late Rev E. J. Nelson, and I remember, particularly, a team of four 'Poddle' Cockers that were handled by Miss Wykeham-Musgrave. These were great fun to watch.

Field trials can still be very enjoyable today and in this computerised age it is good to know of one job that is never likely to become mechanised. I hope that I never see the day when a robot handles a spaniel! Gun-dog training is too personal a thing for this, and therein lies its charm. And so after all the advice, I can only reiterate that understanding as well as skill is the key to successful training, and end as I began by saying, 'Please handle with care.'

125

# IN CONCLUSION

*Know your dog*
Get to know your puppy intimately by studying all his reactions as closely as possible. Thus, if one has the necessary interest and perception, one should be able to assess his temperament correctly.

*Woo your dog*
If the puppy is a shy one be prepared to lean over backwards to gain his confidence.

*Be thorough*
Never try to run before you can walk properly where training is concerned. Teach each lesson thoroughly, and in the right sequence, and do not be tempted to skip things or to hurry.

*Retrieving first*
Train your spaniel so that he is a thoroughly reliable retriever before he sees game and knows the joy of hunting.

126

*Command clearly*

Be sure that your words of command are distinct and that your puppy has a clear understanding of what is required. If in doubt, give him the benefit, but insist on known orders being obeyed.

*Be consistent*

Try and give all your orders in a tone of firm, but quiet, authority. Be consistent in your behaviour, in the words of command, and in your actions and signals.

*Show enthusiasm*

Remember that in training all dogs respond according to your enthusiasm, or lack of it.

*End happily*

Always try to end each training lesson on a happy and successful note, so that the puppy returns to his kennel in the right frame of mind.

*Avoid distractions*

Give him all his early lessons in a place of quietude.

*Concentrate*

Give your dog all your concentration throughout his training and be prepared to be adaptable.

*Allow time*

If there is any doubt as to your having the necessary time to complete a training lesson properly do not attempt to start it.

*Don't daydream*
Remember that 10–15 minutes of concentrated effort is infinitely more beneficial than 2 hours of wool gathering.

*Get together*
When your puppy reaches the pen stage of training take him for a brief, slow, walk on the lead before each lesson. This is in order to 'collect' him, so that you have his entire concentration on you.

*Vary the ground*
Once your puppy is a sound retriever, and proficient at hunting, try and vary the locale etc so that his training is more interesting.

*Keep practising*
If your dog is successful in his first season at field trials do not be too complacent about it. Give him plenty of practice the following summer so that he maintains this standard.

*Keep learning*
If you are fortunate enough to make your dog a field trial champion retrace in your mind the things you did throughout his training in order to achieve this success. In fact, try to learn something from every dog you train, because none of us can claim that we know it all.

# INDEX

*Figures in italic denote illustrations*